"She smokes like a fish"

Unconsidered trifles collected over many years

by

Rex W Last

(Second expanded edition – the Editor's Cut)

ISBN 9781520675213

Cover image drawn by Aidan McKelvie, aged eleven

'My father named me Autolycus; who
being, as I am, littered under Mercury, was likewise
a snapper-up of unconsidered trifles.'

The Winter's Tale, W. Shakespeare

Table of Contents

Author's note

This second edition of *She Smokes like a fish* is dedicated to increasing the funds of a vital national charity, Guide Dogs, Perth Branch, Scotland. All the royalties from sales will be donated to this excellent cause, which depends entirely on private funding. Please read the Foreword by the local Chairman, Deirdre McVean, for more information about their wide-ranging work.

I would be grateful if you could also spare a moment to look at my website www.locheesoft.com which describes the fiction and study skills eBooks I have published on Amazon, together with an account of myself and my life in academe and publishing. If you are fascinated by family history, click on the cover image for *Cursing the Darkness* and then on the link to the background of the book for an account of a very remarkable story from my own relatives' past.

Thanks to grandson Aidan McKelvie for his piscatorial picture on the front cover, to his brother Loghan for the drawing in the Headlines chapter, and a special thanks to my wife Oksana for once again proofreading and making suggestions for improvements. This has been a particularly daunting task in a book largely about mispirnts, sorry, misprints.

The quote at the beginning of the Introduction is taken from the title of the German book *Es fängt damit an, dass am Ende der Punkt fehlt* ('To begin with, there is no full stop at the end'), a remarkable collection of unintentionally humorous handwritten letters and communications with officialdom published by Deutscher Taschenbuch Verlag.

Rex W Last

Foreword

Guide Dogs is a charity dedicated to providing independence and freedom of mobility to thousands of blind and partially sighted people across the UK. There are currently around 4,800 working guide dogs and the owner pays only 50p for their dog! The guide dog service receives no government funding and depends entirely upon public support.

The cost of care, training and maintenance of one guide dog from birth through to retirement is over £50,000, and that is just for one dog. As we promise to provide a guide dog for as long as it is safe and suitable as a means of mobility, a guide dog owner may have up to eight dogs in their lifetime. This means that the cost of that lifetime promise could be well in excess of £400,000.

If having a guide dog is not the best option, Guide Dogs will help people find other ways of achieving mobility and independence such as using a long cane or having a sighted guide. This latter goes under the name of My Guide. Around 180,000 blind or partially sighted people in the UK never leave home alone, and having a guide dog, being a long cane user or having a sighted guide can help compensate for loss of vision.

The Guide Dog service, often through its volunteers, tries to raise awareness of the services on offer and tries to clarify misconceptions. For example, many people think that an individual has to be totally blind to qualify for a guide dog. The fact is only 3% of guide dog users are totally blind. The Guide Dog service also takes an active role in educating the public about good eye care. This is frequently achieved through the network of volunteers giving presentations to schools and community organisations.

Guide Dogs has a vast number of volunteers across the UK. Currently there are around 14,000 volunteers who do work that is worth around £28 million per year. There are so many different roles for volunteers, from becoming a puppy walker, a boarder, a driver, a speaker, a campaigner or a fundraiser.

Perth and District Branch of Guide Dogs actively seeks to promote all the aspects of the work of this charity and we firmly believe in what Guide Dogs sets out to achieve. We are dedicated to fundraise at every opportunity which is why we are delighted to have the support of Rex Last and look forward to working in partnership with him.

With the expansion of the service to include younger and older people, the costs of operating the Guide Dog service continues to grow year on year. As we frequently tell people who put spare change in our collection boxes, 'Every penny counts.'

Deirdre McVean Volunteer Chairman Perth and District Branch Guide Dogs (Scotland)

Introduction

To begin with, there's no full stop at the end – comment on a student essay

I have always been fascinated by language and its perversities. It all began with my name, Rex Last. I was brought up in Suffolk, where this surname is by no means unusual. There must have been a load of cobblers working in those parts to allow the term for their principal tool to become such a common surname in East Anglia.

I've often been asked if I am related to James Last, the composer and conductor, who sadly passed away as I was revising this chapter. My response is, 'Unfortunately, not.' That particular Last was a famous bandleader from Germany, which for him was troublesome in a different way, as 'die Last' is the German for a burden, and that was also a source of some sly amusement among my students. My own name has also been a burden for me in more ways than I care to mention. Here is just one example.

I dread ringing up call centres to place an order for goods, because I know it will eventually lead to the apparently straightforward issue of my name and address. Finally (or should I have said 'at last'?), we get to the point. The operator asks in shaky English: 'What is your last name?' When I reply, 'Last,' the tired but patient voice at the other end of the line says, 'Yes, *last* name, sir. What is it?' At which moment I know we are in for a long and unproductive exchange. I persist in proclaiming my identity, and the operator persists in repeating the question on the script before them.

As for my first name, Rex, this has a noble origin as it derives from the Latin for 'king'. When I asked my mother why I was given this name, her reply was, 'Because you can't muck about with it.' Mother, have I got news for you. Apart from a little three-letter word it rhymes with, my name has been taken in vain by a dinosaur, Tyrannosaurus Rex, and it acquired contemporary fame in the name of the popular singing combo T Rex. The name appears in various other locations, in the toilet product Andrex, for example and more recently in the 2016 referendum on the European Community in the word 'Brexit'.

One of the more unusual variations on my Christian name came in a bill from my gas supplier who unsurprisingly was unable to read my handwriting. It was addressed to: 'Rev W Last.' That could, I guess, be described as a holy original error. I have lost count of the number of times 'Last' has been transmuted into 'List', 'Lost' and, worst of all, 'Lust', but, to quote the words of Francis Urquhart from *House of Cards*, 'I couldn't possibly comment' on the appropriateness or otherwise of that 'last' misprint.

More recently, I received a letter from Currys PC World inviting me to subscribe to some expensive enhanced guarantee deal or other, which begins: 'Dear Baron Last'. Words fail me. At least it wasn't spelled 'barren'.

Such perversions of my name contributed greatly to my becoming fascinated with the vagaries of language in general and its vast potential for misunderstandings in particular.

This collection of unconsidered trifles came into being many years ago when I was a Lecturer in German at Hull University. Apart from being famous for having its own local telephone service with green and cream phone boxes and an evil-smelling fish glue factory which used to make its presence felt when the wind blew from the wrong direction, Kingston-upon-Hull still boasts a daily paper which used to go by the confusing name *The Daily Mail*, because it is actually the evening paper for the locality. It has no connection with the London morning paper of the same name. To avoid confusion, I have rebaptised the paper as *The Hull Daily Mail* in the rest of this book.

I was inspired, if that's the right word, to start the collection by a small item printed on the front page of that paper in December, 1975. In those days, the Hull to York road was a well-known single-track highway with a large number of accident black spots, and my eye caught the report of a fatal crash in which firemen had to cut the body free. The item ended with these jaw-dropping words:

> Firemen from Market Weighton released the body. The dead man is believed to live in the area.

On the main notice board of the Department of Scandinavian Studies at Hull University, I chanced upon another item which further inspired my search for more assaults on the English language. It was a large yellow poster for Uppsala University summer courses for 1977, which I spirited away while no one was looking and added to my hoard. Here is the interesting bit:

Main building of Uppsala University.

History does not record how many students flooded to Uppsala that summer as a result of such an irresistible promise. The mistake is understandable, as 'sex' is actually the Swedish for 'six'. Honest. Scandinavian languages are rich in such potential international confusions. Here is just one more instance: in Danish, 'fart-kontrol' means nothing more sinister than 'speed check'.

Little gems like that tend to cause a fleeting smile then vanish without trace, but I decided to try and preserve some of them for posterity, without any clear idea of what I might eventually do with them. To this end, I began collecting press cuttings and other material which disappeared into a cardboard box many years ago and which I have only recently unearthed. Fast forward to the new technological era of the eBook, and that offered me the opportunity to bring these faded flowers out into the harsh light of day.

This book is a selection of those scattered bits and pieces which I have gathered over the years. But this is not just another mishmash of misprints regurgitated from the pages of dozens of other books of howlers and boobs and clangers and the rest, most of which are tediously familiar or quite frankly completely unfunny.

There will of course be the occasional item which you may have encountered before, but most of this material comes straight from the pages of the press, the loudspeaker of my radio, or some other direct source. And the centrepiece chapter on malapropisms is entirely original, as it contains a substantial collection of foot in mouth utterances from a departed colleague who had the gift of scrambling his vocabulary in a quite remarkable way, and in the process unwittingly gave me the title for this book.

It's all in the title

The manly Art of Knitting – book aimed to encourage real men to take up the needles

Now and then an absolute gem slips through the net (to mix a metaphor), and I start off with some of the very best I have encountered. First up, appropriately enough, is a fishing magazine title which, I kid you not, appears on the magazine shelves with monotonous regularity. Maybe it's just me, but I simply have to pick up this magazine each time I see it to check that the title is for real and not just some awful misprint:

Now for a trio of genuine book titles from the shelves of recent acquisitions in Hull University library back in the 1970s, the first of which has to be read out loud (but not too loud) for best effect:

Everybody's Pepys

Modern Movements in Architecture

Competition in the Sausage Market

How the second one in particular slipped past the eagle eyes of the editorial team is beyond belief.
Now for one title that I really didn't credit until I saw it on Amazon's website in all its glory, which means it must be true:

Cooking with Poo

The unusual surname comes from Thailand, and I assume the

chef concerned washed her hands first. If you think it can't get better, you are wrong. There is actually a pair of children's cookbooks entitled:

Cooking with Pooh

The Pooh Cook Book

The reference is, of course, to Winnie the Pooh. To top it all, there really is a book:

Quick-fix Cooking with Roadkill

And while I was earnestly researching this material, I came across the best Country and Western title for a book ever:

I still miss my Man but my Aim is getting better

All these titles are genuine, as is the following which, I am assured, is aimed strictly at cat lovers:

Games you can play with your Pussy

A debunking account of the life and times of Mother Theresa by Christopher Hitchens really is called:

The Missionary Position – Mother Theresa in Theory and Practice

Another unfortunate title, this time an English translation of the adventures of an outstanding Luftwaffe pilot in World War Two, Heinz Knocke, goes like this:

I flew for the Führer

And scratched his eyes out?

I end with the titles of a few novels which maybe should have been reconsidered:

For Dick's Sake

Kissing the Rod

Mr Sterling sticks it out

The lively Fanny

Many of the above fall into the same unfortunate category as the apocryphal *Biggles flies back to Front* and *Biggles flies undone*.

In other words, if in doubt, do please try and choose a less ambiguous title.

Down to business

Lord of the Fries – sign over a fish and chip shop

Everyone starting up in business is on the lookout for an eye-catching name, logo and slogan, however, not all of them are entirely successful, and quite a few of them inadvertently fall flat on their face. One local example in our nearby town is the hairdressing salon with the name:

Curl up and Dye

A quick trawl through the Internet reveals that other coiffeurs have employed the same turn of phrase, but it's not one I would have chosen. Names like the following, from hairdressing and elsewhere, strike me as less open to challenge on grounds of taste, although a couple of the puns are pretty awful:

A Cut above

Hair we go

Facial Attraction

British Hairways

Sheerlock Combs

Jack the Clipper

Scissor's Palace

Overcome with Emulsion

The last item on the above list is a genuine decorating business based in London. You can check out their website if you feel so inclined.

There also really is a beauty salon called:

Hand Job Nails and Spa

And, whether you believe it or not, there actually is a pet

grooming establishment with the mind-boggling title:

Doggie Styles

And there are many more with far less printable names than that, ones which make the Knobs and Knockers section of the local department store sound quite innocuous.

If you are in search of an ironing service, there are a couple I can recommend:

Ironing Bored

Iron Maiden

A village not far from where I am writing has a large shop front displaying the name of a company which specialises in gardening and landscaping products, and I am sure the owner didn't realise the spooky implications of splitting up the name differently from his original intentions:

Groundscare

There is an antiques and furniture dealer with this rather uninviting name:

Junk and Disorderly

And I came across a witty individual who had given his ink refills for computers business this natty title:

Alan Cartridge

In nearby Dundee I spotted a roof repair service under the name of Dynasty, with a deliberate pun in its slogan: 'Dinnae stay under leaky roofs'. For non-Scots, 'dinnae' means 'do not', and 'to stay' is the equivalent of standard English 'to live'.

Here's an itchy example from a Professor of German at Cambridge who told me that as a young lecturer in London he would pass by a garage every day quite happily until he realised the awful alternative significance of the name of the company above its main doors:

The Crawley Body Works

Street names are often fraught with danger as are unfortunate signs like this one near a retirement home in a quiet cul-de-sac:

Dead end

Naturally, house builders seek out the most distinguished designations they can for their upmarket developments. Names like Railway Cuttings and Factory Lane are strictly off the menu, but occasionally in their search for sophisticated names for developments targeted on the discerning upwardly-mobile executive purchaser, they can still fall flat, as this painful-sounding address indicates:

Wyllie Court

– which reminds me of the Second World War story of the packed underground train that suddenly comes to a halt and all the lights go out. In the darkness, a loud American voice enquires, 'Is this Cockfosters?' Embarrassed silence, then a stage whisper could be heard in reply, 'No, it's mine.'

Moving swiftly on, Borough Green Parish Council did not anticipate the protests from a gay couple who took offence at a street named after a local councillor. Bangways Way was, the objectors claimed, unsuitable and inappropriate. The Council turned down their complaint. Perhaps they could have renamed it as Wilde Drive, as was proposed for one thoroughfare in Reading?

One of my favourite road signs is to be found on the Edinburgh bypass. The turn-off to Ikea is at Straiton Junction, and if my wife is not looking, that's what I do: go straight on.

Back to witty and not so witty business names. The following list has been dredged up from a variety of sources, and I begin with a septet of variations on the boring but much less confusing 'Fish and Chip Shop':

A Salt and Battery

Chip n Dales

Frying Nemo

Lord of the Fries

The Frying Scotsman

The Codfather

A fish called Rhonda

The last offering was found over a shop in Treorchy, Wales.

Many brave attempts at puns are less than successful:
Florist Gump

Planet of the Grapes

Flush Gordon

Napoleon Boiler Parts

Leaky Lou

Wear Abouts

Indiana Bones Temple of Groom

Boris' Carloft

Pita Pan

Amazing Grates

Tyred and Exhausted

Wok around the Clock

Buckingham Pallets

Sofa so Good

One respectable Dutch publishing company has such an inappropriate name that I have to reproduce their imprint just to prove it really does exist:

The company apparently specialises in scientific titles like the enticing *Multivariate Analysis in Vegetation Research*. Its advertisement goes on to claim that it publishes no less than 18 Junk journals. No comment.

And finally, how would you introduce this individual? 'You must be – Joe King'.

Typos

God does not make misteaks – Wayside Pulpit

My own writing career began way back in the days of hot lead letterpress, with clanking machinery, galley proofs and all the paraphernalia of that venerable technology. It was not long before I became familiar with the pitfalls of getting into print. I recall being mortified that my very first set of proofs for an article in the academic journal *German Life and Letters* came back with the phrase 'he baldly states' corrupted into 'he badly states'. Fortunately the blunder was made good before the article was released into the wild, but that gave me an early insight into the huge potential for mistakes lurking on every printed page.

I was able to make the necessary correction, but no such happy fate befell a distinguished colleague of mine in the Scandinavian Studies Department. He had sweated and laboured over the first sentence of his key chapter on a famous Swedish playwright and finally came up with this beautifully crafted formula: 'In all the lumber of Strindberg's works...' Regrettably, the subeditor (presumably acting in the role of a pre-electronic spellchecker), thought better and the sentence came out limply as 'In all the number of Strindberg's works...'.

The processes of academic publication tend to function at glacial speed, which at least offers the time for most blunders to be eradicated, but the commercial magazine business faces radically different challenges. Editorial staff spend their days furiously chasing a constant stream of weekly or monthly deadlines which are a fertile breeding ground for all manner of errors large and small. Stand by for a fairly crass example.

For some time, I freelanced as editor of the official Amstrad PCW computer and wordprocessor magazine in an open plan London office where many other titles occupied the vast floor space, one of which was the prestigious monthly *Amiga International*. The Amiga was an early upmarket desktop microcomputer. On one of the page proofs for the news section of this particular issue the editor had keyed in a holding caption under an image reading 'Type some shit in here please', but no one actually obliged before it appeared in print. As I recall, the editor just about survived that particular disaster, despite the fact that the offensive four-letter word was by no means as inoffensive in print then as it is today.

Even greater pressure is placed upon those working in the daily press, and one of their number, *The Guardian*, is notorious for the wealth of misprints which stalk its pages. The problem was compounded by the fact that in its earlier days the paper was based in the provinces and called *The Manchester Guardian* (for pretty obvious reasons). The first edition pages were sent down to London to be printed, and naturally they contained the largest number of typos. To be fair, there were probably no more typos in the early edition of *The Guardian* than in other newspapers, it was just that the earliest and most error-prone edition was the one most widely circulated.

Here is a selection from its pages: a report on the pop group 'Ian Dury and the Blackheads' rubs shoulders with a film called 'Chariots of Fir'. So that's what those racing two-wheelers were made of. The paper also succeeded in renaming a London borough as 'Hammershit', and there was a gleeful item from our crime reporter about a bunch of criminals on whom 'the police ponced'. I've always wondered what 'banged to rights' meant. (For much younger readers, the pop group referred to above was actually 'Ian Dury and the Blockheads'.)

Typos have a long and distinguished history and as far as I can determine, one of the grandaddies of them all was the so-called *Wicked Bible*, which revised the seventh the Ten Comm-andments as 'Thou shalt commit adultery.' Moses was alleged to have said when he came down the mountain for a second time: 'The good news is that I have got them down to ten; the bad news is that adultery is still in.' And the worst news, I guess, is that according to the *Wicked Bible* it's also compulsory.

Typos come in a wide range of different flavours. Apart from a lack of skill in spelling which results in those all too common blunders, like 'grammer', 'neccessary', 'definately', 'cemetary', and many more, one prevalent form of typo nowadays arises with the inappropriate substitution of a word not recognised by the spellchecker with what it thinks is a 'correct' word.

The errors generated by the predictive text feature of mobile phones and other devices are too humorous to mention (as someone once put it), and they can be seriously annoying when the word you are typing is grabbed by the system and rendered as something else. Examples are legion and many may well be invented for effect: 'biros' becomes translated into 'birds', 'crosscountry' morphs into 'crossdressing', and so it goes on. If you google the phrase 'predictive text' you can enjoy a cascade of such howlers which for my taste rapidly become very unfunny and contrived.

But perhaps the worst category of error is the word which the spellchecker recognises as being correct in its dictionary, but it's embarrassingly wrong for the context. One of my prized possessions is the British Rail Humberail timetable for 1977-78 which contains the following useful little note: 'The information shown in this folder is subject to alteration, especially during Pubic Holidays.' That's a case of one little omitted letter which makes an 'L' of a difference:

Nafferton	d.	19 01		20 00								
Driffield P	d.	19 05	19 42	20 05	21 42	21 58				10 04	12 10	13 0
Hutton Cranswick	d.	19 10										
Arram	d.	19 18										
Beverley P	a.	19 23	19 55	20 17	21 54	22 10				10 17	12 23	13 1
Beverley P	d.	19 24	19 56	20 18	21 55	22 11	22 20	23 25		10 18	12 24	13 1
Cottingham P	d.	19 30	20 02	20 25	22 01	22 18	22 26	23 31		10 24	12 30	13 2
Hull P	a.	19 38	20 10	20 32	22 09	22 25	22 34	23 39		10 32	12 38	13 3
King's Cross †	a.			03u01						15 19		17 2

The information shown in this folder is subject to alteration, especially during Pubic Holidays.

Humberail, by the way, was the name given at that time to the region north of Hull, the line to Scarborough, where it is claimed all the old diesel trains went to die.

That particular embarrassing omitted letter is not an uncommon slip and there is a possible explanation for it provided by this quote from the *Yorkshire Post*. Apparently, it's a result of cutting back on the word 'public':

> Mr Basnett would have the Government restore public expenditure cuts in order to create new pubic sector jobs.

There is a duller but more plausible explanation which lies in the location of the letters 'p-u-b-l-i-c' on the keyboard, which makes it likely that the touch typist could accidentally miss out the 'l', and that would also explain why 'solider' is a frequent mistyping of 'soldier'. In that case, the finger of the right hand can easily hit the 'i' key before the left hand finger gets to 'd'. But perhaps I'm being too kind to the typist.

One further example of the fateful missing letter which I cannot resist concerns the Yorkshire farmer, a typically blunt and outspoken individual, whose two daughters were attending an expensive public school. The headmistress sent out a circular letter to parents regretfully announcing an increase of fees to a much larger sum 'per anum'. Although not an individual of great learning, the farmer could readily spot a mistaken request for money, so he responded to the headmistress that he would 'prefer to continue paying through the nose in the normal fashion'. The correct spelling of the phrase is, of course, 'per annum', per year.

Less serious, perhaps, but far more common, are grammatical blunders like confusing 'there' with 'their', 'its' with 'it's', and 'your' with 'you're'. However, the most toe-curling category of typos occurs when an unfortunate newspaper attempts to correct a mistake and in so doing introduces an even more embarrassing lexical car crash. You may have come across my two favourites in this category.

First, the adventures of the curiously named General Pillow (who was almost certainly not the inventor of pillow fighting). The *Burra Record* reported that he was 'bottle scarred', and then compounded the felony by printing an apology to the effect that the phrase should have been 'battle scared'.

And the second is a priceless gem from the *Ely Standard*: 'We apologise for the error in last week's paper in which we stated that Mr Arnold was a defective in the police force. This was a typographical error. We meant of course that Mr Arnold is a detective in the police farce, and we are sorry for any embarrassment caused.'

Yet another category is that of malapropisms, which we shall be examining in depth in a later chapter.

Strange but true

Under the surgeon's wife – report about the assassination attempt on President Reagan

Sometimes human logic defies belief, as in this report in *The Hull Daily Mail* of a woman who had sent her son off to the local motorcycle races with a pack of sandwiches. When she discovered that the meat in them was bad she contacted the police, as she was concerned for his welfare. The boys in blue leapt into action, located the lad and asked him to contact them if he felt ill.

The last line of the report reads:

> A police officer said, 'And we have heard no more from him which we regard as being a good sign.'

Here's the full text of the report:

ALERT OVER MEAT IN BOY'S SANDWICHES

A HESSLE WOMAN telephoned Bridlington Police station yesterday afternoon to say she had given her 15-year-old son meat sandwiches to take with him to the Carnaby motorcycle races and that she had since found that the meat was bad. Could they contact him and stop him eating them?, she asked.

Police traced the boy, but by this time he had eaten the sandwiches. "He said he would let us know if he began to feel ill," a police officer said. "And we have heard no more from him which we regard as being a good sign."

What really puzzles me is (a) that the mother did not realise until much later that the meat was bad and (b) that the police interpreted silence on the boy's part as a positive indicator.

As you will have seen, the above item also contains a couple of misprints, 'Palice' and 'bay', neither of them quite as disastrous as the impact of the whole story.

Next, a radio report on the ever-interesting topic of the logic of trade unionists stated that it was not fair that shopworkers had to work on Sundays. They should, it was argued, be allowed Sunday off – so that they could do their shopping. There is a logical flaw lurking in there somewhere, surely.

Also on logically shaky ground was the sign in the KFC window in Surrey, which announced: 'Open seven days including Sundays'.

A gem, this time from *The Daily Telegraph*, which I am assured wasn't published on 1 April, stated that:

> Teams of environmentalists have been posted along the autobahns of southern Germany to help frogs and toads cross the busy carriageways from their winter quarters to spring breeding grounds.

Further down, the article refers to 'black spots' on the road, presumably along with large numbers of skid marks:

> Most of the major roads and autobahns in South Germany have black spots where the motorway divides frogs' and toads' winter quarters from their spring breeding grounds.

One more strange report, again in *The Daily Telegraph*, tells of a department store shopper holding up a pair of underpants and asking if they would fit someone with a size sixteen and a half collar. I presume those were extremely long johns.

Same paper, another dodgy story:

> Officers called to reports of a reptile on the loose found a 'venomous adder' that was 'lying very still on a patio' at a block of flats... Officers then made inquiries at the flats, only for a resident to reveal that it was a garden ornament. A local man, Gary Hollins, 43, said: 'I could have told you it

was a fake snake because the paint is peeling off it.'

And when President Reagan was shot, a foreign English language newspaper reported that he was 'under the surgeon's wife'. Which reminds me of the reporter who allegedly asked Abraham Lincoln's widow immediately after his assassination, 'Apart from that, Mrs Lincoln, what did you think of the play?'

Another surreal presidential moment came from a source which I can no longer recollect, but it's well worth quoting. Michelle Obama appeared at an event in a sleeveless dress, and the commentator noted:

> The First Lady demonstrates the right of Americans to bare arms.

There is also the alleged account, which Dr Spooner would have loved, of a huntsman out in the wilds of America who was attacked by a brown bear, and in the mêlée, the bear grabbed the man's rifle and shot and wounded him. As one wag pointed out: That demonstrated the right of Americans to arm bears.

Another daily paper claimed paternity for an impending royal birth with the splendid headline and byline:

> Princess Beatrix Pregnant
> (by our Royal Correspondent).

Or perhaps that should be Royal Co-respondent?

Not long ago, a Sky News reporter informed us that the Duke of Cambridge was embarking on a new career 'as an air ambulance pirate' (hopefully without a patch over one eye). The Duke himself compounded the felony in the interview that followed, in which he said that 'this job will keep me grounded'. That's rather like the man who took up cycling because it would 'keep me off the streets'.

And this caption is rather unkind to the Duke of Edinburgh:

THE DUKE
'Man obsessed with material benefits'

The text, if it's too grubby to make out, reads 'The Duke – Man obsessed with material benefits'.

There are some unfortunate notices which may or may not be true, but which have the ring of authenticity about them. One I particularly like was claimed to have been seen pinned to the door of a seaside fairground booth:

Gypsy Rose Lee. Closed due to unforeseen circumstances.

Until I mislaid it some years ago, I had long cherished a photograph of a country scene in the Lake District, with the following prominent notice:

Public conveniences – over the bridge.

Another confusing rural sign caught my eye, this one warning of the dangers of gambolling:

Do not drive fast young lambs.

Our local Tesco store has a large sign hanging from the ceiling of one of the aisles with the following mystical legend:

WATER SPIRITS

I looked, but I couldn't find any. Then there are the signs in the clothing section for Menswear, Womenswear and Childrenswear – far too much swearing for my liking.

And one more sign, this one invented but amusing enough, is alleged to have been found on the gates of Venice:

> Beware of the Doge

(For more than a thousand years, 'Doge' was the title of the chief magistrate of Venice, and is related to the Latin 'dux', which means 'leader'.)

But you don't have to make them up. Reality can be truly strange enough. This item was found lurking in the *The Daily Telegraph*:

> A Spanish civil servant who failed to turn up for work for six years was only discovered when he was considered for an award for loyal service.

To end this chapter, the following bizarre item from the 1960s is also entirely genuine and was published in the original Spanish. I believe it appeared in the *The Guardian*. Here is an English translation:

> To compensate for a deficit in its finances, the Society for the Protection of Animals of Barcelona has organised a bullfight.

Epitaphs

I knew this would happen – an American gravestone

This is, I must confess, the least original section in the book, but we are all heading towards a situation in which we might well need an epitaph to record our passing, so here are some choices for you to consider.

By the way, why is it when someone unexpectedly shuffles off this mortal coil, it always seems to be an individual of impeccable character, a pupil loved by all his or her friends, a keen scholar, an outstanding sports enthusiast, a loving husband or wife and mother, a great businessperson and so forth? It never seems to be the case that the deceased is a no-hoper, constantly bunking off school, a failure at everything they turned their hands to, a solitary figure much hated by his or her contemporaries. Whatever happens to them? Do they live for ever?

Most folk are content with a purely descriptive gravestone coupled with a succinct phrase summing up the dear departed. The problems begin to arise with the epitaph itself, which can be wide open to misunderstanding as in the case of the wife who had these ambiguous words engraved on her husband's headstone:

Rest in peace. Until we meet again.

Or, to be cynical, perhaps that is exactly what the lady meant.

Quite often, a touch of humour is injected, presumably to allay the pain of loss. Some of the best are one-liners like the following which can apply to any composer you care to name:

Now decomposing.

And here are some more, including a couple by well-known individuals:

Die? That's the last thing I'll do.

You should see the other guy.

I told you I was ill (famously Spike Milligan, but used by others).

Here lies an atheist – all dressed up and no place to go.

His sins were scarlet but his books were read (Hillaire Belloc's choice of epitaph).

And my own personal favourite in this category:

Live burial world record attempt.

Then there are the verse offerings, like this proposed but unused ponderous farewell to the seventeenth-century architect and dramatist John Vanbrugh:

Lie heavy on him, Earth, for he
Laid many heavy loads on thee.

Next, we turn to the strangely credible couplet for a departed seaman:

Here lies the body of Jonathan Ground
Who was lost at sea and never found.

And let me sneak in this alleged farewell for a village postmistress:

Returned unopened.

My most cherished epitaph story bears a close similarity to the words attributed to John Wayne, as he stood at the foot of the Cross in some interminable CinemaScope Biblical epic. In his accustomed drawl, he delivers the line, 'Truly this was the Son of God.'
'Cut!' cries the producer. 'John, say it with awe.'
John duly obliges with: 'Aw, truly this was the Son of God.'
And here is the epitaph story which it parallels. A Yorkshireman asked the stonemason to engrave on his wife's tombstone the words: 'She was Thine.' Shocked to discover that the mason had carved 'She was Thin', he demanded that the missing 'e' be inserted forthwith. On returning later to the churchyard, he went up to the stone and read, 'E! She was Thin.'
Another unusual epitaph was this apparently innocuous piece of

verse on a Montreal tombstone:

> Free your body and soul
> Unfold your powerful wings
> Climb up the highest mountains
> Kick your feet up in the air
> You may now live forever
> Or return to this earth
> Unless you feel good where you are.

It's harmless, that is, until you realise that this is in fact an acrostic, a poem in which the initial letters of each line spell out a word or phrase. I leave it to you to work out what that expletive from beyond the grave is.

The burial of two significant figures in dramatic history forms the essence of this apocryphal graveyard story. A reviewer, drawing on the dispute between those who were convinced that Francis Bacon wrote Shakespeare and those who believed the Bard himself was the rightfully acknowledged author, commented that a particular performance of a Shakespearean drama was so dire that the authorship of the plays could be put beyond doubt by opening up the coffins of Shakespeare and Bacon and finding out which of them had turned in his grave. The reviewer was W S Gilbert of Gilbert and Sullivan fame, referring to the Hamlet of Arthur Bourchier, a sometime actor and theatre manager.

And, on the subject of a real historical figure, there is no truth in the rumour that the parking fine for Richard III's remains in Leicester has been doubled as he was found lying across two spaces.

That gives me the excuse to digress for a moment to record two more short and pointed reviews. The first is a terse assessment of a theatrical performance of the play *I am a Camera*:

> No Leica.

The other is of the tragedy of *King Lear*:

> He played the king as if someone was about to play the ace.

Back to epitaphs and related topics, we turn to an entirely

fictional case.

Imagine a solemn meeting of the Horse Whisperer's Association lamenting the passing of a colleague and remembering his demise in the execution of his duties. But, as the Association President, put it, 'He was determined to move on to greater challenges, and for us he will always be known as – the Lion Whisperer.'

I wonder what the epitaph might be? Pride comes before a fall, perhaps.

And to round things off, here is a genuine simple epitaph text consisting 'only of an initial and a surname hinting at the consequences of a misspent life on earth:

P Burns.

To which there is no answer.

Lifting the Iron Curtain

How can you use a banana as a compass? – part of an East German joke (read on for the answer)

Nostalgia, as someone once said, is not what it used to be. And, apart from a handful of diehards or folk who benefited disproportionately from the régime, no one yearns for the days of the Cold War and the Russian empire which held eastern Europe in an iron grip. It was an especially cruel time for German citizens in the Russian zone which became known as the German Democratic Republic. It was neither German, nor democratic, nor a republic. They had just endured the brutality of the Nazi régime and the years of death and destruction wrought by the Second World War and now had to confront decades of repression in a Communist state.

With the passing of those years the political joke aimed at satirising dictatorships and their political systems has also tended to disappear off the map. Here are some which you may not have come across and which I have unearthed for you to enjoy.

The human spirit somehow manages to rise above the most challenging of circumstances, and in the GDR it responded with a deeply ironic and embittered strand of humour. GDR jokes, unsurprisingly, tend to be in the original German, so I have translated a selection of the best of the bunch.

While on the topic of bunches, this comment on the lack of foreign fruit sets the scene:

> 'How can you use a banana as a compass?'
> 'Put it on the Berlin wall. The side with a big bite out of it points east.'

Erich Honecker was the leader of the GDR from 1971 until just before the fall of the Berlin Wall in 1989, and he features in large numbers of humorous tales. In one of them he is claimed to have promised the famous GDR ice skating champion Katharina Witt to fulfil any one wish she may have. She replied that he should open the Berlin wall for one whole day.

> 'Cheeky girl! So you want us to be all alone, just you and me?'

Another story, which I have heard in a number of variations, goes something like this: Two men are sitting together in a tram in the city centre and one asks the other: 'What do you think of Honecker?'

His companion, deeply alarmed by the question, replies: 'Shhh!'

As the tram moves out into the suburbs, the question is repeated and the same response given.

Finally, the tram reaches the terminus on the city boundary and the second man indicates to the first that they should get out and take a walk along a secluded woodland path. Once in the depths of the country and far beyond human habitation, the second man says: 'Now you can repeat your question.'

'So what do you really think of Honecker?'

A long pause, then: 'Well, actually, he's not that bad.'

Another joke making Honecker a figure of fun goes like this: he is asked by an old lady if Karl Marx was primarily a scientist or a worker. Following the party line, Honecker replies that he was first and foremost a worker.

'That makes sense,' says the old lady. 'A scientist would have tried his theories out on rats first.'

Now for the best-known Honecker joke of all. One morning, Honecker gets up and greets the sun. 'Good morning, Mister Sun.'

The sun replies: 'Good morning, Comrade General Secretary and Leader of the State Council of the German Democratic Republic.'

At midday, Honecker greets the sun again. 'Good midday, Mister Sun'.

The sun replies: 'Good noontime, Comrade General Secretary and Leader of the State Council of the German Democratic

Republic.'

In the evening, Honecker greets the setting sun. 'Good evening, Mister Sun.'

'Sod you,' replies the sun, 'I'm in the West now.'

And now for another rather clever Honecker story. Our Leader finds himself in a Soviet spaceship orbiting round the earth. The spaceship suddenly develops a serious fault and threatens to go out of control, fall out of orbit and burn up as it enters the earth's atmosphere.

An angel knocks on the window of the spaceship and says: 'If you shout out "Long live Capitalism", I will rescue you and deposit you safely down on mother earth.'

Honecker, good Communist that he is, refuses.

Other systems on the spaceship fail and the situation becomes even more perilous. Again the angel appears at the window, makes the same offer, but Honecker stoically refuses to concede.

Yet more systems break down, and the stricken craft spirals earthwards through the atmosphere. As the whole ship begins to glow from the blistering heat of re-entry, the angel appears for a final time, again making the same urgent plea: 'Call out "Long live Capitalism" and I will pluck you from the spaceship and deposit you safely on the surface of your home planet.'

Desperate and close to death, Honecker shouts out 'Long live Capitalism', to find himself being roughly shaken by the comrade sitting next to him, who says, 'If you must talk in your sleep during a Party congress, make sure you do it quietly!'

On a different topic, a serious break-in has taken place in the Ministry of the Interior. Honecker rings the Chief of Police, and asks, 'Anything important stolen?'

'Yes, sir. The election results for the next five years."

In Heaven, Honecker's guardian angel begs for time off, as he is totally exhausted.

Saint Peter says, 'Surely you can't be so tired, as you are only protecting one man?'

The angel replies, 'But I'm protecting him from 17 million people.'

And finally on the subject of Honecker: Just before the collapse of the GDR régime a press report announces that Honecker had been shot fleeing to the West. But not in the back.

Another well-kicked butt of GDR humour was the Trabant, the most famous and notorious industrial product of the GDR, for which potential purchasers had to wait months or even years. It was a noisy and smelly two-stroke, two-cylinder car of which over three million were produced. One later version incorporated a VW engine. The name means 'companion' or 'satellite'.

Apart from familiar stories which were also directed against earlier versions of the Skoda (like 'How do you double the value?' Answer: 'Fill the petrol tank') many Trabant-specific jokes have entered the history books, like this one: 'A new Trabi has been launched with two exhaust pipes – so you can use it as a wheelbarrow.'

Now for a real classic. A customer orders a Trabant car. The salesman tells him to come back to pick it up in nine years. The customer: 'So shall I come back in the morning or in the afternoon?' The salesman: 'You're joking, aren't you?' The customer replies: 'No, not at all. It's just that I need to know whether the plumber can come that afternoon or not.'

Here are some more selections from the almost unlimited supply of Party jokes.

Two work colleagues discuss attendance at a Party gathering. 'Why weren't you at the last Party meeting?'

His colleague replies, 'If I'd known it was the last meeting, I would certainly have been there.'

Next, Stalin (or any other dictator in the Eastern Bloc you care to name) summons his Chief of Secret Police and angrily tells him that his watch has been stolen.

An hour later, Stalin rings up the Chief of Secret Police to apologise, stating that he had simply mislaid the watch and that the search should be called off.

'Impossible, Comrade Chairman,' replies the Chief. 'Forty-five people have already been arrested and twenty-eight have confessed to the crime.'

Next up, another watch-related tale. Three groups of workers at a factory are facing punishment. The first lot turned up late, and were accused of idleness and lack of commitment. The second lot turned up early, and were accused of being spies. And the third lot turned up on time. They were accused of secretly buying watches from the West.

Three dogs meet, one from the glorious Soviet Union, one from the People's Republic of Poland and one from the German Democratic Republic.

The Soviet dog says, 'Every time I bark, I get a piece of sausage.'

The Polish dog says, 'What's a piece of sausage?'

The GDR dog says, 'What's barking?'

The Huber family have bought a parrot. Unfortunately, the only words the bird can say are: 'Damned Communist swine! Down with Honecker and all his gang!'

One day, a local Party bigwig comes to visit the family and in a panic they hide the parrot and its cage in the freezer.

After the man left, they rush to the freezer and extract the shivering creature. 'Brilliant Communist Party! Honecker is the hero of our country!'

'And why,' asks the father of the family, 'have you changed your tone so radically?'

The parrot responds: ' Two hours in Siberia is quite enough for me.'

One comment on that joke: They actually had a *freezer*? How bourgeois.

A war widow has a parrot which her deceased husband, who had served in the Navy, gave her as a present. Regrettably the parrot was addicted to swearing about the GDR régime, so she put a cover on the cage on a Sunday in order to have one day of rest, not least because she had retained some of the Christian values of her parents' generation.

One Monday morning, she has just taken off the cover from the parrot when a senior party official comes up the drive. He enters the house just as the widow frantically covers the parrot again, and he hears the muffled voice squawking out: 'It's been a bloody short week! Down with Honecker!'

A third parrot story (why so many parrot stories, I wonder?): A citizen rings up the local People's Police and informs them that his parrot has escaped from its cage and is currently flying around the locality.

'And why should we need to know about that?' asks the duty officer.

'Because,' answers the frantic citizen, 'you need to know that I do not necessarily share its political views!'

Every year the GDR arranges an annual festival for the best political joke. First prize: 'Five years in Siberia.'

And now a couple of stories about border guards on the Berlin Wall, which was known officially in the GDR as the Antifascist Protection Wall, not that too many citizens in the West were keen to break into Eastern Germany.

One border guard says to the other: 'What is your view of the GDR?'

His colleague replies: 'The same as yours.'

The first guard: 'Then I am going to have to arrest you.'

Here comes border guard story number two:

First border guard: 'What would you do if the Berlin Wall suddenly collapsed?'

Second guard: 'I'd climb that tree over there.'

First guard: 'Why on earth would you do that?'

Second guard: 'I don't want to get killed in the rush.'

One of the wittiest Communist political jokes I have come across is the following about the Stasi (Stasi = Staatssicherheitsdienst, the East German state security police).

A GDR citizen walks through the streets of East Berlin at night shouting out: 'Shitty state, shitty régime!'

A Stasi officer appears and arrests him. The citizen demands to know why he has been arrested, because he hadn't indicated which state and which régime were shitty.

The Stasi officer thinks for a moment, nods thoughtfully and releases the man.

Ten minutes later he runs up to the man and arrests him again.

'What now, why are you arresting me this time?'

'I've just realised that there is just one shitty state and one shitty régime. You're nicked.'

And an attack on the Party top brass at large:

Every day, a citizen purchases the *Neues Deutschland* (New Germany) newspaper at a local kiosk, scans the first page, and then throws the paper away.

After some days, the newspaper vendor says, 'Forgive my curiosity, citizen, but why do you buy *Neues Deutschland* every morning, scan the first page and then throw the whole paper in the bin?'

The citizen replies, 'Because I want to read the death announcements.'

'But,' counters the vendor, 'death announcements are on the back page.'

'Well,' says the citizen, 'the ones that interest me are on the front page.'

Now a couple of definitions:

> Can you explain to me what capitalism is?
> Capitalism is the exploitation of man by man.
> And can you explain what Socialism is?
> The exact opposite.

What is a quartet?

> A GDR symphony orchestra after a tour of Western Europe.

And finally: For some years the East German Post Office received numerous complaints that a new one-Mark stamp bearing the face of Honecker the President would not stick on envelopes. After thorough investigations it was found people were spitting on the wrong side.

Headlines

Monty flies back to Front – Daily Mirror (referring to General Montgomery in World War Two)

One of the most challenging problems facing journalists and subeditors alike is how to squeeze as much meaning as possible into the smallest number of words. This frequently occurs in what's appropriately known in the trade as 'body copy', the main text of a report or article. John Smith is never just 'John Smith', he is 'local gardener John Smith, 35, divorced, four children, of 22 Railway Cuttings', and his pet dog isn't just 'his dog', it's 'a three-legged Alsatian, with a black mangy coat and one eye missing, answers to the name of Lucky'.

Nowhere does this information overload have such potentially disastrous results as in the headline, which often ends up by saying a lot more than intended and totally confusing the reader.

Here is a mixed bag of examples, most of them drawn from *The Hull Daily Mail, Driffield Times* and *The Daily Telegraph* over a period of years. We begin with a potential new use for the bagpipes:

Scottish oil piped ashore.

You have to read the full article to discover that this next offering is actually about Flamborough Head, just north of Bridlington, but it's a good enough illustration of the ambiguous headline to quote here:

Hands off Head councils tell County.

But why should one church swap its main musical instrument with another?:

Church approves organ transplants.

I hope the result here was a clear round:

Olympic rider jumped lights to save horses.

But in what way do these ladies of the night attract His Holiness?:

Prostitutes appeal to Pope.

Here's the lead-in to a tall story about controlling problem urban areas:

52 Foot Officers to patrol violent Neighbourhoods.

At least they will be able to see trouble coming from that height. What was the subeditor thinking about when crafting this headline about the results of a drugs raid?:

Crack found in man's buttocks.

Maybe this next individual was the man who said he would give his right arm to be ambidextrous, but one consolation is that he can still use chopsticks:

One-armed man applauds the kindness of strangers.

And now, an intruder finds that his way into the top floor window has become a bit of a tight fit:

Husband went up drainpipe with hammer.

It appears that Catholic priests can now marry, so long as they love each other:

Church leaders in marriage talks

THE Archbishop of Canterbury, Dr. Coggan, left for Rome yesterday for talks with the Pope on a number of subjects —including inter-marriage between Catholics and Protestants.

When Dr. Michael Ramsey, the former Archbishop of Canterbury, visited the Pope in 1966, mixed marriages were one of the problems causing most difficulty.

Roman Catholics can now get a dispensation from their Bishop to marry a Protestant, and the Catholic party has only to undertake to try to bring the children up as Catholics.

News of the discussions aroused more speculation that the Prince of Wales might be planning to marry Princess Marie Astrid

Dr. Coggan talks to Mgr. Benelli at the start of his Rome visit

Where else would deficiencies in the water supply be found?:

More water restrictions in pipeline.

We appear to be suffering from an invasion of holidaying junkies:

> Visitors from abroad shoot up as outlook for economy gets sunnier.

And, let's face it, drugs are everywhere nowadays:

> £10m acid Plant Aid is Shot in the Arm for Hull, says MP.

Change is taking place one millimetre at a time:

> Britain inches grudgingly towards metric system.

This sounds like an odd case of aversion therapy:

> Hooked on the Internet? Help is just a click away.

It's not clear exactly what is going on here, but apparently the rider was unhurt:

> Horse bounces off car roof.

And now a perfectly reasonable attitude on the part of a group of workers (this may require more than a moment's thought):

> Miners refuse to work after death.

Assailants occasionally resort to unusual weapons:

> Knife youth attacked girl with pushchair.

Here is a sinister turn of events. It seems they're now pointing missiles in our direction:

> Chinese scientists aim for Britain.

Next, what appears to be an interesting example of interspecies polygamy:

> Man offers 50 cows to wed Obama's daughter.

English cricket is so desperate that they are recruiting the kitchen staff to help out:

> Cook set to become England's highest test scorer.

Just so long as his culinary efforts give his team the runs, I suppose.

Here is a message from beyond the grave explaining why people who have been murdered are unwilling to come forward:

Homicide victims rarely talk to police.

Next, ten from that all too common category, the hopelessly ambiguous headline:

Potato shortage cuts chips in half.

Shark cancels surf event.

Girls head suspended.

Cabinet ministers turn on Thatcher.

Vandals strike at works site.

Nun, 35, expected at court.

135 cadets in Sandhurst passing out.

Last chance for legless cat burglar.

Ski school slips up on sacked instructor.

Thatcher's twin
aims for Tokyo.

The last headline was actually split over two lines, which makes it all the more intriguing. I assume the reference isn't to her children Mark and Caroline, who are actually twins.

Next, a nautical selection, courtesy of *The Hull Daily Mail*. Apparently, the local fisherfolk still use sailing ships:

Blow for Hull Fishing Fleet.

And the paper came up with two impressive foot in mouth headlines which had a colleague of mine requiring oxygen when I showed them to him. First, a nocturnal encounter with the Icelandic fisheries protection vessels:

Night of rough Rammings off Iceland.

The territorial squabbling between the UK and Iceland over the rich fishing grounds to the south of the country came to be known as the Cod War, and the next headline sounds even more unfortunate than it looks (with its allusion to an item of attire for gentlemen in the first Elizabethan age):

Tight lips all round on cod peace moves.

Unsurprisingly, this front page lead was hastily reworded in later editions.

The somewhat vulgar undertones of that headline were unintentionally echoed in a story about an RAF station which was keenly anticipating the appearance of a young lady celebrity. She was obliged to cancel the engagement, and the unfortunate headline writer expressed the grave tidings in these words:

Miss World blow for RAF men.

They wish.

This next offering reflects a farming practice from the past which is no longer tolerated, namely, the burning *in situ* of the remains of the grain harvest, which used to cause all kinds of problems for vehicular traffic on country roads, but could read like a penalty for the infringement of dress code or untidy appearance:

A local law about stubble.

This reminds me of a gem from the *Herne Bay Press* on the same subject:

The season for grass fires seems to have arrived, so stamp out that cigarette-end before you throw it down.

Now for a couple of 'finds' which turn out to be deliciously ambiguous, the first from the *Fife Herald*, the second is of unknown provenance:

Hillwalkers found safe.
Man found dead in cemetery.

We turn now to a selection of headlines which are as puzzling as they are unintentionally humorous:

Bugged bra case optician wins fight.

Lollipop sacking goes to court.

A proud father's snaps.

Stole weasel after stag party.

Calls for cat judge to be vetted.

Disappointment as the Stones miss Dundee.

Chewing gum saves bonfire from tractor.

This advertisement for specialist workers is a real conundrum – does it mean that you have to dress yourself in heavy duty underwear to be employed in Germany?:

Wire Drawers
required to work in Germany.

Is this confused item about bad golf players or what?:

Her clubs help stroke victims.

And now, to prove that the criminal fraternity never overlooks an opportunity:

Thieves pull off socks raid.

That is rather like the alleged report that all the toilet seats had been purloined from the local police station, which concluded with the official statement that 'police officers have nothing to go on'. Or the case of dogs stolen from local kennels: 'Police are anxiously looking for leads.' Or again, a lorryload of Merino sheep, famous for their wool, escape from a crashed lorry: 'Police are still combing the area.'

The next headline apparently appeared in *The Sun*. A lunatic escapes from the asylum, enters a laundromat, assaults the women, and flees:

Nut screws washers and bolts.

And finally for this chapter, do be careful what name you choose, especially if you are contemplating going into politics. This headline is fictional, but legend has it that it appeared in *The Times* in relation to Michael Foot's leadership of a committee on nuclear disarmament:

Foot heads arms body.

The local town of Blairgowrie just down the road from where I am writing often has its name abbreviated to 'Blair', usually when referring to the local football team. Visitors to the town must have been baffled by all the attention the then Labour Prime Minister Tony Blair was getting in the *Blairgowrie Advertiser*, not all of it good news, it seems:

Blair braced for a big chill.

Defeat was never an option for Blair.

Brave Blair a spot unlucky.

Blair left out in the cold again.

Blair hopes are still high.

And one further item I came across seems to indicate that, far from repenting his military incursions into Iraq, he intends to go on to ever higher things:

Blair's plans to fly with the Saints.

At least Foot and Blair don't have a name like that of the leading Labour politician who lost his seat in the 2015 elections: Ed Balls. Now that is a real gift for the headline writers.

More headlines

Bank employee retires – Driffield Times

The Times newspaper, way back in the day when it was a broadsheet with small ads on the front page and printed on quality paper so shiny it would cause your fish and chips to slide off, had a reputation for seriously understated headlines. I cannot recall the exact wording, but one famous example went something like this:

> Small Earthquake in Chile
> Not many Dead.

Local newspapers, with little of note to report, are often left trying to achieve the opposite, in other words, inflating trivia to the level of an international incident. I start with a prize example from the *Driffield Times* which actually made the front page lead in what can only be described as a very, very slow news day:

> Watering cans vanish from cemetery.

Another equally dull main headline from the same source would hardly merit a mention in the national press:

> Resident of the Limes, 87, dies after bath.

On the occasion of a Mr Wilkinson's retirement, he is photographed in *The Hull Daily Mail* under this caption (my question is: What happened to the other one?):

> 37 Years with one Firm.

Local press often boldly tells life as it is, in all its stark drama:

> Bank employee retires.

> Bridlington man moves up Ladder.

> Prompt action by Mayor saves Sheep.

Did the sheep say, 'Thank ewe?'

Here's another headline which accidentally turned out to be about as tasteless as it gets:

Court told of brothel in Madeley-street.

The problem was that this report was set right next to five prominent pictures of happy couples in the Weddings of the Week section, as you can see from the badly faded original:

THE DAILY MAIL, TUESDAY, MARCH 8, 1977   5

MAN JAILED FOR 'TOUTING'

Court told of brothel in Madeley-street

Mr Gerard Gribben and Miss Patricia Carfill, pictured outside Holy Name Church, Hall-road, Hull after their wedding.

Not just headlines, but reports too, can contain eye-watering trivia, like this item from the Women's Institute:

> The mystery competition was for the heaviest handbag, and was won by Mrs Metcalfe.

Another meeting which must have drawn a huge crowd included a competition for three scones and an amusing and interesting talk by Mr Arnell entitled, 'It happened to me'.
And at a different event, 'Miss Watson gave a talk on tea towels.'
It sounds like this could have been an even more uncomfortable session:

Edwardes to meet unions on sacking?

I'd prefer soft cushions myself. The gentleman with the oddly-spelt name was chief executive of British Leyland during the worst strike-torn years of the British motor industry.

A different local paper stated that people had been invited to a local hall 'to meet councillors and beat police officers'.

The next duo of headlines are apocryphal but ought to be real, the first containing a glorious misprint:

Poof reader required for *Gay News*.

Young lady required for milking.

They lead me on to this final item which was found lurking among the classified advertisements in the *The Dundee Courier*, back in the days when the paper was in broadsheet format and the front page was given over to small ads. My theory was that this was to prevent people too mean to buy a copy from reading the headlines from other passengers as they sat in the train or bus for the daily commute. The notice read:

Schoolboys and girls required for planting.

Perhaps they would grow into hothouse plants?

Nil illegitimi carborundum

Caesar sic in omnibus – a line which can be mistranslated as 'Caesar was unwell on the bus' instead of 'Caesar thus in everything'

Crusty old academics like myself may bewail the fact that Latin and Greek have more or less vanished from the curriculum of our schools, becoming doubly dead languages, but there is no denying the fact that Latin continues to have a pervasive influence in many aspects of everyday language.

In present-day English, you can find it lurking just about everywhere. But don't worry, I'm not about to expatiate on this *in extenso* (at length).

One fascinating aspect of Latin is the way it still hangs around in church language and in mottos and logos, as well as in a whole range of common phrases and abbreviations, which can be very easily – and sometimes wilfully – misunderstood, as the following will show. I have set the Latin in bold, the mistranslation next, followed by the correct version in brackets:

Ars gratia artis – 'You scratch mine and I'll scratch yours' (Art for art's sake, best known as the logo of Metro Goldwyn-Mayer).

Stabat mater – 'Matricide by knife' (short for Stabat mater dolorosa, the grief-stricken mother [Mary] stood [at the foot of the Cross]).

Bona fide – 'Give the dog a bone' (in good faith, genuine).

Per ardua ad astra – 'It is difficult to buy a Vauxhall' (Through struggles to the stars, motto of the RAF).

Sic transit gloria mundi – 'On Monday, Gloria was unwell in the van' (Thus passes the glory of the world).

Abusus non tollit usum – 'Do not misuse the toilet' (Misuse does not cancel out correct use).

O Fortuna – 'O for tuna', the song of the unlucky sea

fisherman: (properly rendered as 'O Fortune', the famous opening chorus of Carl Orff's *Carmina Burana*).

That last item in the list reminds me of the greetings card sent to the incompetent oil prospector: 'Get well soon'.

The title of this chapter – 'Nil illegitimi carborundum' – is actually a made-up phrase which roughly renders into English as 'Don't let the bastards grind you down'. Another amusing mistranslation comes from 'Morituri te salutamus' (We who are about to die salute you, the greeting by gladiators in the ancient Roman arena before the fighting began), which has been mischievously mistranslated into English with the help of two Old Testament towns:

Sodom, for Gomorrah we die.

There are any number of echoes of Latin and Greek language in our present-day culture. Take the name of Prometheus. He was the man who in Greek mythology stole fire from heaven and, as a punishment, was tied to a rock where his liver was pecked out every day by an eagle. He was, as has been pointed out, the first person to experience the slogan 'freshly de-livered daily'.

If you are interested in the phenomenon of 'surface translation', an international way of scrambling language, you'll find the cod Latin poem 'Caesar adsum jam forte', from which the title quote to this chapter is taken, in a variety of places online.

There are two other notable illustrations of this perverse application of language skills in French and German books of English nursery rhymes. The German text is called *Mörder, Guss Reims*, and the French *Mot d'Heures, Gousses, Rames*. Both render the English title *Mother Goose Rhymes* into equivalent-sounding words in the target languages.

The French book has a rather neat attempt at 'Humpty, Dumpty', the first two lines of which go like this:

Un petit d'un petit
S'étonne aux Halles

– which is the surface translation of:

Humpty Dumpty
Sat on a wall.

The French means 'A little one (i.e. child) of a little one was surprised at Les Halles'. Les Halles is the former covered fresh food market in Paris, replaced by a new construction in 1971, with yet another upgrade currently being built.

Cut off in my prim...

Dress offers from House of Fraser plus top off... – an unfortunately abbreviated email title

I have recently come across a whole new area of possibilities for error with the help of the email program on my iPad. It merrily truncates email names and addresses in order to fit them in to the narrow column space allowed, but instead of sensibly cutting off in between words, the words themselves can become sliced in two, sometimes at the most inappropriate junctures.

Here is a selection gathered over the past months of these electronic feet in mouth, beginning with a worrying communication from a building society:

Your Nationwide current account state...

Is dire? Beggars belief? Not at all: as you may have gathered, it's just that the word 'statement' is sawn in two by the program. The next offering leaves me wondering if it really is an unfortunately truncated word or not:

Thank you for your email. We have received your mess...

Presumably it was in a sealed plastic bag.

Reports on Amazon book orders also throw up (no pun from the previous item intended) some interestingly retitled items:

Your Amazon order of The Stud...

Your Amazon order of A German Win...

Your Amazon order of How Man...

The first is actually *The Study Skills Handbook* (honest), the second *A German Winter*. The last one could well be *How Manufacturing evolved in Europe* or *How Mankind faces the Future*, but it's actually a fascinating book about popular mathematics entitled *How many Socks make a Pair*.

Lastly from Amazon, a very unfortunate word split indeed:

You can reach more readers by putting your tit...

The reference is to the title of your book and where you could put it, so to speak.

For some reason, my wife's emails from House of Fraser have ended up in my Inbox, with the following alluring invitation:

Dress offers from House of Fraser plus top off...

Just in case that baffles you, the line should conclude 'plus top offers'.

Recently I noticed that the Mac computer tends to compress filenames not by chopping them off at an arbitrary point, but by removing the middle section of the name, so the file I am currently working on comes up on screen as:

She smokes like...Rex W Last

On the wider topic of word mutilation, the omission of a single letter can cause all manner of confusion, as in the phrase 'my awful wedded wife'. Added letters also have unintended results, as in the letter from a parent to a head teacher asking for the child to be excused 'as he has the flue'. Call the chimney sweep.

Or note the manner in which this word mutates: 'A mistress is halfway between a master and a mattress.'

Another way in which you can scramble language is by forming an anagram from one or more words. There is a website dedicated to anagrams in all shapes and sizes (which can also be used for crossword cheats like me who need help solving clues), www.wordsmith.org. It contains The Anagram Hall of Fame, and here are just a few gems from a huge list of their appropriate anagrams:

Clint Eastwood = Old West Action

Western Union = No wire unsent

The Morse Code = Here come dots

Mother-in-law = Woman Hitler

And as a long-suffering computer programmer, this is especially true:

software = swear oft

If my own name, Rex W Last, is put through the anagram mangle, it libellously comes out as:

Trawl Sex

I wish to register a complaint.

Ecclesiastical blunders

Any member of the congregation who enjoys sinning – A magazine announcement encouraging new voices (or was that vices?) for the choir

It's bad enough when professionals try and get their copy into shape, but when amateurs are let loose on anything from posters to larger publications, the results can be doubly disastrous. Nowhere is the situation more fraught with peril than in the field of church communications, in particular parish magazines.

Maybe those of a religious persuasion are purer than the rest of us and tend not to see a *double entendre* or two for our grubby little minds to pounce on with undisguised glee.

The situation is compounded by the fact that the words 'son', 'sin' and 'sing' crop up often in these circles and hamfisted typists struggling away on their computer keyboards frequently get them muddled up:

> The senior choir invites any member of the congregation who enjoys sinning to join the choir.

> The rosebud on the altar this morning is to announce the birth of David Alan Belzer, the sin of Reverend and Mrs Julius Belzer.

Other notices with unintended howlers have a delightful naiveté about them. Try these three on for size:

> Bertha Belch, a missionary from Africa will be speaking tonight at Calvary Memorial Church. Come tonight and hear Bertha Belch all the way from Africa.

> Sermon this morning: Jesus walks on the water. Sermon tonight: Searching for Jesus.

> A bean supper will be held on Tuesday evening in the

church hall. Music will follow.

Which reminds me of the delightfully irreverent complaint from a fisherman on the Sea of Galilee:

'I don't care who your father is, you're not walking where I'm fishing.'

The next note from a parish magazine is not for those of a nervous disposition. Avert your eyes now:

The ladies of the church have cast off clothing of every kind. They may be seen in the basement on Friday afternoon.

Be careful what you decide to choose as a song, or you may find yourself in trouble:

Miss Charlene Manson sang 'I will not pass this way again', giving obvious pleasure to the congregation.

A lot of interesting things are going on below stairs in this parish:

For those of you who have children and don't know it, we have a nursery downstairs.

Here are a couple of announcements of forthcoming events which are so bizarre they just have to be true:

Low Self-Esteem Support Group will meet Thursday at 7 to 8:30pm. Please use the back door.

Weight Watchers will meet at 7pm. Please use large double door at the side entrance.

And I was actually present when a local vicar, trying to allay fears that the church's central heating might fail, reassured us with these immortal words:

If the central heating fails we can fall back on the electric fire.

The unintentional foot in mouth

One of the main causes of tooth decay is plague – Stirling Observer

The various organs of the media are gifted at saying one thing and meaning another, and I offer here a selection of related feet in mouths, again gathered over years of collecting newspaper cuttings and various other scribblings. On the subject of organs, by the way, 'Bach's great organ works' is a classic LP. It certainly did work, as appropriately for a composer he had a score of children. Now I rapidly change the subject and get down to business.

Much of the fault for howlers lies within language itself. We have at our disposal a limited number of letters of the alphabet, a restricted range of vowel and consonantal sounds and a huge amount of different notions, concepts, ideas, descriptions and more to cram into them. A lot of the skill in speaking and understanding language lies in our ability to make the right assumptions about the sounds we make and hear, and the shapes we write and read. However, the opportunities for confusion, amusing or otherwise, abound. Consider this apparently harmless sentence:

He opened the door in his pyjamas.

This sounds perfectly reasonable until you add the thought, 'What a strange place for a door.' And, in turn, that makes the following statement even more intriguing:

He shot the lion in his pyjamas.

Now that you are in the right frame of mind, the next comment will certainly strike you as biologically challenging:

I didn't recognise little Johnny. He's grown another foot.

The simplest form of this kind of howler is an illogical scrambling of events and the order in which they happen:

Three alcoholics who killed another man and then cut up his body into pieces, while he was still alive, were sentenced to life imprisonment.

And another offering in the same vein is a BBC news report about a coup in Kenya, which refers to an individual who:

> died in the fighting, together with a West German woman who was married to a UN official and a Japanese tourist.

Busy girl. This is as muddled as the local paper report:

> Youth ran at pal with carving knife.

I myself would be tempted to run in the opposite direction.
During the Falklands war, a front line BBC news reporter stated mysteriously:

> They could see the Argentinian soldiers eating their sandwiches through binoculars.

And an item from Radio 4 gives an insight into the joys of plastic surgery:

> The modern woman of today is fortunate in being able to pick her own nose.

Another radio news broadcast from 1982, before the wrong kind of leaves or snow were invented, but with a similar search for excuses after some minor meteorological disaster, went like this:

> We hope to be running trains on more or less the same lines as usual.

Next, a real flat foot in mouth, a statement of the obvious: reporting on a raid at Lloyds Bank, the BBC informed us:

> Police believe thieves are responsible for the robbery.

That is cutting edge detective work at its best.
Here's the BBC again in 1977, banging on about Britain investing large sums on insulation and energy saving:

> In its determination not to lag behind other industrialised

countries...

Oh dear.

Sometimes the most innocent turn of phrase can be easily misconstrued, as in this delightful extract from Jane Austen's *Northanger Abbey*. Here she is describing her heroine Catherine Morland emerging from tomboy to young lady:

> At fifteen, appearances were mending; she began to curl her hair and long for balls.

Equally innocent in its intent is the billboard announcing the departure of a stage coach (they were often given the names of nobility) from a public house in Scotland:

> The Duchess of Atholl leaves the Duke's Arms every morning at eight o'clock.

There was a famous baseball player called Yogi Berra (now there's a name to conjure with) who almost falls into the category of making dumb jokes, but there is a strange kind of logic to his utterances, for example:

> You should always go to other people's funerals, otherwise they won't come to yours.

That reminds me of the footballer who asserted:

> If my manager stands behind me, I'll stand behind him.

Eurosport Channel onscreen listings recently included the following odd item. Perhaps these two tennis players have talents the rest of us have not been informed of:

> 11.45 Cycling - Murray v. Djokovic

Here's a report from a local news broadcast about a woman who wasted away and died weighing just a couple of stone:

> It was said that she was extremely emancipated.

And an advert in the *Bookseller* for a *Dictionary of Battles* includes a reference to the Yom Kipper War (Just in case: that should read Yom Kippur, the Day of Atonement in the Jewish Calendar.)

A Scottish railway trade union official, speaking about potential industrial action by his members, recently asserted on the Scottish TV news for the BBC:

> We stand up for our passengers.

Haven't we been doing the same for you for far too long?
The *Stirling Observer*, ever concerned about the nation's health without being all that clear as to what causes what, reported in 1981 that looking after your teeth is important and stated:

> One of the main causes of tooth decay is plague.

Someone should erect a plaque to that.
Here's a rather intriguing small ad from a New Zealand newspaper, the *Waikato Times*:

> Help with pregnancy. Phone xxxx.

I tried the actual number but it was engaged. Several times.
Well done, BBC North news, you have found the real culprits for a blaze:

> A fire at an old people's home has been treated as arson by the police.

Or, as an unfortunate copper allegedly put it, 'There's a lot of arson about.' (That really needs to be spoken out loud for full effect.)
Another local newspaper contained a report on brave firefighters rescuing a cow from a bovine predicament. It had become stuck in a mud patch but the intrepid officers rescued the poor beast, and the reporter stated: 'They deserve a pat on the head.' Oh, really?
It's not too often that issues arise because of regional differences, but there is one splendid example from Lincolnshire which nearly resulted in a collision between a tractor and a diesel train because of a linguistic misunderstanding.
The sign at the crossing read:

> Do not cross while red light is flashing.

In standard English, that's as clear as a bell, but unfortunately in the local dialect 'while' means 'until' as in, 'I won't see thee while Thursday'. I leave you to imagine what nearly happened next.

Advertisements provide a steady stream of unintended blunders. A favourite of mine is a current TV advertising campaign targeted at follicly challenged gentlemen:

> Belgraviacentre.com specialises in nothing but hair loss.

I think I'd be a little more impressed if they specialised in hair gain.

Now for a trio of business adverts which need no additional comments:

> Tattoos done while you wait.

> Unexpected vacancy for knife-thrower's assistant.

> Four-poster bed 100 years old. Perfect for antique lover.

This pair of adverts in the Jobs Wanted section makes offers which couldn't possibly be misunderstood:

> Man, honest. Will take anything.

> Tired of cleaning yourself? Let me do it.

And a warning to all reporters: don't interview children. One brave fellow tried on the *Today* programme in 1979, and the exchange went something like this:

> Interviewer asks small Rhodesian child: 'What differences have there been at your school since coloured children have been coming?'
> Child: 'Everything's the same.'
> Interviewer: 'In what way is everything the same?'

To which there is no answer.

A visit to the doctor can often bring about an unintended exchange, as in this situation, which I am assured was genuine. A lady of mature years appears in the consulting room and tells the doctor that her left leg is hurting:

> 'That's caused by old age, Mrs Jones.'
>
> 'Well, my right leg is the same age and that isn't hurting.'

My own doctor had an even better response. When I told him my arm hurt when I lifted it like this (ouch), his reply was: 'Don't lift it, then.' Another doctor-related mis-statement occurred to a friend of mine a long time ago when she was being anaesthetised for an operation: 'You will now feel a little prick.' No comment.

Many amusing blunders are caused by the ignorant pomposity of officialdom. A colleague in the Russian Department of Hull University told me that when living in Wales he was a little baffled to receive a communication from the local authority in response to his request to build a shed behind his house:

> I am happy to inform you that you have permission to have an erection in your garden.

My colleague wondered if he should go out on a balmy summer evening and think of nature and the infinite vastness of the universe. Perhaps that would do the trick.

A nice round but rather pointless number is reported in *The Daily Telegraph*: 'The first clash came after about 0 members of the Southend branch of the Socialist Workers party were barred from reaching the hall by a squad of police.'

Now for an interesting snippet from a report on Sky News: 'In cities, it's collisions between cycles and lorries that are most fatal.' Presumably other kinds of deadly collisions are only slightly fatal.

I turn next to more blunders which underline how important it is to read the instructions, however ambiguous they might be. Here are a handful of offerings which may require more than one reading for the underlying double meaning to emerge:

> Stir well before use.
>
> Keep away from children.
>
> Stand in a warm place.
>
> Pierce film in several places.

Nothing sucks like an Electrolux.

Nothing acts faster than Anadin.

So, in the case of the last example, take nothing?

Which reminds me of the radio report that 'workmen are replacing cats' eyes on the M6.' Personally, I don't think it will catch on.

One scandal which has been puzzling me for some time is the so-called plebgate saga, in which a distinguished Conservative politician was accused of abusing a policeman at the gates of Downing Street. However, I think I have discovered what was really behind it. Apparently, according to the *Mail Online*, Andrew Mitchell MP had been through a 'long and extremely frustrating day', which included lunch at the Cinnamon Club, London's poshest curry house. He insisted on leaving via the main gate, but the police officers would not let him through:

> After several refusals he eventually made his way to the side gate, where he let rip at officers.

That's what upmarket curry will do for you. No wonder the police officers were upset.

As you may have gathered from the beginning of this book, I am no friend of call centres. One particular message which annoys me is the canned voice saying 'We are experiencing long waiting times.' No you are not. *We* are experiencing long waiting times.

Now for a livestock-related story told to me years ago by the Director of the Adult Education Centre in York. He was also a lay magistrate, and one of the trickier cases he had to adjudicate involved a farmhand who stood accused of having unnatural relations with a pig in a barn. The leading witness was another farmhand who had observed the proceedings through a gap in the wall. The magistrate demanded of the witness to explain why he had not intervened, and the reply came:

> That weren't my pig.

A foreign offering caught my eye with this sign in a carpark in

Germany:

> Ladies parking. Leave five spaces free.

Does that mean for *each* lady?

To conclude, an intentionally humorous foot in mouth which I rather like, a small ad in the General Vacancies of *The Hull Daily Mail* in 1976:

> Clerk, £25 plus. How about this for a life of ledger? – Brook Street Bureau.

As someone once said, a Freudian slip is when you say one thing and mean your mother.

What's in a name?

I name this ship 'Dammit I just cut my finger on the bottle' – entirely invented expletive from a launch ceremony

One of the most difficult tasks parents face is naming their child, and ensuring that the first name does not clash with the surname. The two most well-known cases of such unfortunate combinations are Pine Coffin and Albert Hall, but there are many, many more. I attach a selection of some of the more printable ones I have encountered:

Olive Hoyle

Justin Case

Dick Staines

Bob Sherunkle

Fanny Payne

Willy Stroker

Ann B Dextrous

Ben Dover

Cy Kosis.

Jean Poole.

Morty Fide

Mrs Sippy

Vy Brator

Jimmy Riddel

If the significance of the last name in the list eludes your grasp, think Cockney rhyming slang.

And, to round them off, two offerings which may take more than a moment's thought, but they are pretty unfortunate for the poor individuals who have to go through life as:

Sue Perman

Terry Bull

Also, do be very careful whom you marry. The advertisements in what are affectionately known as the Hatch, Match and Dispatch sections of the newspaper usually put the surnames of the bride and groom together, often with unintended results:

Best – Lay

Flynt – Stone

Seeman – Sample

It reminds me of the BBC and its bureaucratic love affair with acronyms, which in this particular case landed them in some trouble. It seemed reasonable to abbreviate the Service Engineer as SE, and the same applied to the Regional Service Engineer (RSE), but their luck ran out with the Assistant Regional Service Engineer (er...). Presumably he – or she – provided a back-up service.

There is a lovely French story, which thankfully does not lose much in translation, about an individual with an unfortunate name who presents himself before the magistrate with what appears to be a quite reasonable request. First, in case you require a translation, 'merde' could roughly be rendered as 'faeces (vulg.)'. Here he is addressing the magistrate with his request:

> 'My name is Hippolyte Merde, Monsieur le magistrat, and I would like to change my name.'
> 'Excellent decision,' replies the legal dignitary. 'And what name have you chosen to replace your current unfortunate appellation?'
> A pause, then, 'Monsieur le magistrat, I have chosen – Charles Merde.'

One of the best name stories concerns an ancestor of Alec

Douglas-Home (pronounced 'Hume'), whose name allegedly acquired the odd pronunciation because one of his distinguished military forebears, going into battle, sought to rally his troops by shouting out the family name – 'Home!' – which they unfortunately misinterpreted, and so they duly charged – back home.

People are fascinated by names that match the job, like Slaughter for family butcher, Payne for doctor, and so on. The phenomenon has even acquired a fancy title, aptronymns, and researchers into illustrations of such nominative determinism (now there's a mouthful) believe that individuals with a particular name tend to gravitate to a job which relates to it. On my study wall, for example, I have an impressive landscape painting by a local artist. His name: Peter Drewett.

At which point, given my own name, I suppose I should say I must be off now to repair some shoes. The trouble with this theory is that if you choose names and jobs out of two lucky dip boxes, eventually a minority will match, but the overwhelming majority will not.

It's our nature as human beings to find it somehow comforting to see patterns in life where for the most part randomness rules. We say that it is a most significant coincidence that we met an old friend on the train today, and conveniently overlook the huge number of other days when we met nobody.

Names like Cardinal Sin, former Archbishop of Manila, or Mrs Burnham, a domestic science teacher, are amusing, but little more than that. Less amusing, because of the savings lost by so many people in his Ponzi scheme, is Bernie Madoff, who, it's been pointed out, 'made off' with millions of investors' money. He was sentenced to 150 years imprisonment in 2009, and I wouldn't like to be in his shoes when he is released.

Given the extent of the Volkswagen scandal over fraudulent pollution emission readings, it's even more unfortunate that one of the VW board members issuing a statement on the subject should be Olaf Lies.

Here's a genuine advertisement, somewhat tattered, from *The Hull*

Daily Mail which speaks for itself:

R. BODDY

FUNERAL SERVICE

365, Holderness Road
HULL.

Tel. 29327   mtc

My own particular favourite is the family of Dorset builders called Crumblehome, but that's a long way from marking a special bond between name and occupation. If you google the name you will find on their website an explanation of what it actually means.

And who on earth would make a point of undergoing the arduous training to become a urologist with a name like Cockburn? Someone did. There was also a lady called Sara Blizzard who became a northern TV weather girl and a policewoman named Lauren Order.

However, giving a phenomenon a fancy scientific name like nominative determinism doesn't make it true. Shame, though, it would be nice if it were so.

I turn now to a family story about a name which is, believe it or not, quite true. My grandfather was amongst other things a steam engine driver, and one of the stops on the line which he regularly travelled along was the village of Burston, where a famous strike of schoolteachers took place, the longest strike in history, which lasted from 1914-1939.

Grandfather was also a Cooperative councillor who later rose to become a mayor of Ipswich, and because of his political affiliations decided to give his second daughter the names Lucy Burston, in memory of the strike. Everyone called her Burston and she was rather fond of the unique appellation. I did point out, though, that she was very fortunate that the strike had not been in another village near Newmarket with its own railway station, which went by the name of Six Mile Bottom.

One more topic in the choice of names which is often overlooked is that of initials. You may be familiar with the American comedian with the unfortunate initials: W C Fields, but that is a minor infringement compared to a university administrator long ago who signed his memos: G A S Bunker.

Nowadays texting adds yet another dimension to the possibilities of names to embarrass, with initials like OMG or LOL. The most harmless combination of initials and surname can also turn out to be somewhat embarrassing, as in T. Watt.

The biggest initial pitfall befell a young lady who took on her husband's name, only to find that she has surrendered Patrician Olive Ohlsen for Patricia Olive Travers. One useful piece of advice on this topic I came across, which is demonstrated by the last example, is not to give your daughter a middle name beginning with a vowel, as it can be something of a hostage to fortune. Think Beatrice Unice and words like BUN, BUT, BUM and BUG come to mind.

Finally on the topic of names: A colleague had bought his young son a mouse as a pet, and I made the mistake of asking him two questions. The first was: 'What did you call it?' Answer: 'Archimedes'. At which point I should have stopped. Second question: 'Why?' Answer: 'On principle.'

The joys of spellchecking

Speling Reform Asoshiashun – a   genuine nineteenth-century organisation

When the first WYSIWYG (What You See Is What You Get) word processor appeared, it was hailed as the dawn of a new era. It took a little while for people to realise that, despite its undoubted benefits, computer-based text input and editing could bring with it many unexpected problems, including a whole new generation of errors.

The biggest issue is the result of an attempt to get a machine to assist in the very human activity of manipulating natural language.

I came across an anonymous poem about spellchecking online:

> Eye halve a spelling checker
> It came with my pea sea.

The poem, states the author, has been put through the spellchecker and:

> Its letter perfect awl the way
> My checker told me sew.

Such errors fall into a number of categories. This is one of the commonest: if you mistype a word and the word processor finds the result in its dictionary, no change is made, and you are left high and dry with 'stationery' for 'stationary', 'their' for 'there', and, more unfortunately, 'crap' for 'crab'. Now for a notice from an estate agent:

> A particularly specious semi-detached House.

Next, a creepy description of a splendid garment for a special occasion, which sounds like something out of *Harry Potter*:

> A scarlet robe trimmed with vermin.

Quite often, the mistyping can come up with an entertaining but erroneous formulation:

> A bottle of whisky and a bottle of sherry were stolen by a gurgler.

Here a local authority seeks to cast light in the darkness, but its efforts have been distorted by a single mistyped letter in this report:

> Londonderry is spending council money to improve 'the standard of streetfighting in the city centre'.

And one more from an almost inexhaustible list of possibilities, a TV review in the *Observer* which comes up with an unfortunate twist on the perils of passion:

> A belief that love is just a passing fanny.

Even worse, 'passing' could also have been mistyped as 'pissing'.

If you are having lunch in your local public house, I wonder if you would want to eat something from this descriptive heading to a menu:

> bra food

As long, that is, as they are not serving this tasty side dish:

> mushy pees

If you are preparing a pigeon pie for your customer, do you follow this instruction?:

> Coo for fifty minutes.

And you might be wondering if the countryside is turning Jewish, if you come across this delightful blunder:

> orthodox rabbits

Another awkward misspelling in a political news report went like this:

> The President is at the White Mouse.

And a well-known British politician has her state of mind mangled by *The Guardian*:

> Mrs Thatcher was beginning to suffer from metal fatigue.

That's a very appropriate misprint indeed for the Iron Lady.
The next offering really is a genuine typo in a small ad from the *Yorkshire Post* which must have caused quite a few blushes (or even responses):

> Successful businesswoman seeks … female to shave the enjoyable things in life.

Even more unfortunate is the lady undergoing a standard procedure which threatened to turn into a gender reassignment operation:

> Mrs X will be in hospital for testes.

Another alleged mix-up of names came when a doctor stood by a patient's bedside and said: 'So, you are Mrs A?' A horrified pause. 'No, sorry, you've got MRSA.'

However, there is an even more insidious problem which arises when you type one word as two, or split a word up wrongly, both turn out to be correct, but the result creates an entirely distorted meaning.
Here are a few of my favourites:

> secondhand cars you cant rust

> pedigree Alsation pup pies

> relations hips

> surgeons have a greed to operate

> mans laughter

> I slander

Less common, but equally entertaining, are the results of merging two words into one.

> Mother's help required for children and lighthouse work.

And last but not least, there is the danger of the transposed letter. Take the harmless headline about the general practitioner leaving his practice for the last time:

Doctor set for retiral.

One transposed letter, and his reputation could be in tatters:

Doctor set for retrial.

So my advice to those about to rely on a spellchecker is: Don't.

Howlers

We dispense with caution – Sign in chemist's window

We begin, not with a schoolboy blunder, but an actual end of year report by a woodwork master back in the 1960s at the school where I was doing teaching practice:

> He has enjoyed making his stools.

And an even more regrettable foot in mouth once appeared on the student notice board of a University Department of German. A bit of background first: Franz Kafka's surrealist novellas and novels – *The Castle*, *The Trial*, and *Metamorphosis* – all turn metaphors into reality. In *Metamorphosis*, Gregor Samsa is treated like an insect by his family and one morning wakes up to find that he has actually been metamorphosed into one. The essay title on the notice board invited students to explain:

> Why does Gregor Samsa turn into a Beatle?

And even more importantly, was it Paul or Ringo or another of the fab four?

Here comes a foot in mouth from a student essay which makes one wonder if the writer is thinking of a centaur:

> Brigitta rode a horse like a man.

The next offering was claimed to be absolutely genuine, but if it wasn't, it ought to be. A student essay on medieval buildings came up with an unusual use for what I believe is called an arrow slit or embrasure:

> In the Middle Ages they had no widows, so they used slits in the wall.

The inappropriate use of a word or phrase is always good for a laugh. Here is an example from the BBC in 1976:

> In America, there has been a rash of strange illnesses.

So they spotted them, then.

Misunderstanding of the meaning of a word by children is a rich source of unintentional blunders. First, a schoolboy's response to a request to write a sentence containing the word 'benign':

> I'm eight now, but I'll soon benign.

In the same kind of territory, here comes a science question:

> What is a nitrate?
> Cheaper than a day rate.

And here's another splendid childish attempt at a new definition for a word meaning 'exclusion' or 'expulsion':

> Ostracism is hiding your head in the sand.

Your rhea (sic) certainly would still be visible if you did so.

Quite often, picking up the inappropriate meaning of a word can lead to rib-tickling results. There are four seasons in the year, but what are they?:

> The four seasons are salt, pepper, mustard and vinegar.

Another kind of howler is based on a logical misapprehension or the inability to express a notion correctly. Here are two delightful examples:

> The sea has the largest mammals as there's nowhere else to put them.

> The cuckoo does not lay its own eggs.

Most of the time such confusions are merely amusing, but every now and then the results could be potentially disastrous. We start with the little boy who confused two words: 'Mummy and Daddy are going to Scarborough for the weekend. They are terrorists.' The poor lad meant 'tourists' but that blunder took quite a lot of unpicking.

Here are a handful of other blunders with potentially unpleasant outcomes, all of which are caused by a lack of knowledge of a foreign language.

Go to any large public building in a German-speaking country and you'll see the exit sign: 'Ausgang'. No problem there. But in many cases, airport terminal buildings, for example, you'll also see a sign: 'Notausgang'. An English-speaker with minimal German could well end up in bother if a serious situation arises. The German word 'Not' (pronounced like 'note' in English) emphatically does not have a negative meaning. The noun in German signifies 'need', 'necessity', or, in this case, 'emergency.' So 'Notausgang' actually means the complete opposite of what you might otherwise suppose it to mean.

You may well be familiar with these two very well-known examples which operate the other way round, from German to English. The enraged German customer in a restaurant who has been waiting overlong for his main course calls out in fractured English: 'When do I become a bloody beefsteak?'

His question breaks down into two misapprehensions: first, 'bloody'. In German 'blutig' in this context means the equivalent of 'rare' in English. And the odd use of 'become' derives from the quite understandable mixup over the verb 'bekommen' which in German means 'acquire', 'get'. It's the verb 'werden' which means 'become'.

Example number two concerns a German lady sitting downstairs on a London bus. When the conductor approaches her for the fare, she protests in English: 'The Lord above will pay.' A couple of misconceptions here, but pretty substantial ones. In German, the word for 'man', 'Mr', and 'gentleman' is 'Herr'. Unfortunately for the lady, it also translates as 'God', or 'the Lord' and she picked on precisely the wrong meaning. And by 'above' she means 'upstairs'.

Before leaving the German examples, here is a splendid foot in mouth which doesn't translate too well, but here goes. A sign outside a shooting club reads:

Werde Mitglied
Lerne schießen
Treffe Freunde

In English, that's 'Become a member, Learn to shoot, Meet

friends.' The problem is that 'treffen' in German, as well as meaning 'meet', also means 'hit', as in target shooting. I suppose the nearest in English is 'Hit it off with friends'.

Next a duo of French offerings which may be apocryphal, but still make the point. The first concerns Churchill's alleged response to a request for support from France during the dark days of World War Two. It began 'France demande...' Churchill's reply was abrupt: 'France demands? France can wait.' Unfortunately he misunderstood the French. The verb 'demander' simply means 'ask', or 'request'. To demand is 'exiger'.

The second French mishap occurred to Prime Minister Ted Heath, not notorious for his knowledge of the language. In an attempt to explain in French his delayed response to a request, he said 'J'étais dans les cabinets toute la soirée'. Much mirth across the Channel, as 'le cabinet' does have as one of its meanings the equivalent of the government cabinet; 'les cabinets' on the other hand means 'the toilet', to the delight of the French.

If you are touring in Germany, you may feel you don't want to stay at a 'Bad Hotel'. Far from being Fawlty Towers, however, the name refers to a spa either in or near the hotel, from the verb 'baden', which is cognate with the English 'bathe'.

One more language issue, this time a potentially lethal linguistic mantrap from Spanish. The story goes that a lady who became unwell while on a visit to England, but whose command of the language was negligible, was prescribed a bottle of tablets with the instruction 'Take once a day'. Unfortunately, 'once' in Spanish, pronounced 'on-they', means 'eleven'. History does not record what happened to the lady concerned.

As the notice in the chemist's window proclaims:

> We dispense with caution

That howler is upstaged by the sign in a gift shop window in Scotland:

> Long felt wants for sale

It's all because of the Scottish winter weather, I believe. By the way, German visitors may well have given that shop a wide berth, as 'Gift' is the German for 'poison'.

Now for a rather delicate matter. The *Driffield Times* reporter comments with a straight face on the growth of a furnishing company (a least I assume it's a furnishing company):

> The expansion of North Bar Reproductions' premises will be complemented by expansion into other areas of reproduction, with the inclusion of bedroom furniture.

Nowadays, we spend too much of our time avoiding the minefields of political correctness. Even the most innocent of remarks, it seems, can lead to castigation if not dismissal, like the Professor halfway through his 9 o'clock lecture who sternly addresses a young lady student for arriving late:

> We really must go to bed a little earlier, Miss Peabody, mustn't we?

Not long ago, a distinguished visiting Professor of University College London was summarily removed from his post for making an off-the-cuff remark about the differences between men and women which, many folk claim, had the serious blemish of being (a) of humorous intent and (b) not too far from the truth. In the mistyped words of *The Daily Telegraph*, 'Many believe that Sir Tim was sacrificed on the alter of political correctness.' No change there, then.

A pretty tasteless (I use the word advisedly) example of political correctness gone crazy came in a day-long conference at a Scottish City Hall which I attended. Next to one of the trays of lunchtime snacks was a card bearing the legend:

> Non-vegetarian sandwiches

Here's an unfortunately worded poster outside a certain famous towering Blackpool establishment (presumably he will also be playing that other saucy misspelling, 'Penis from Heaven'):

> Come and watch Dennis Waggit at the organ.

On the subject of towering, I wonder if that famous metal tower in Paris, constructed as an embellishment to the 1889 World's Fair, got its name from a group of the organisers discussing it when it was being built, and one of them remarked: 'What shall we call it? It's a bit of an eyeful.'

Now for a few items I have come across which fall under the heading of 'animal crackers':

> Great dames for sale.

> Free puppies: half Cocker Spaniel, half sneaky neighbour's dog.

> Kennel for sale described as very turdy.

> Dog for sale: eats anything, loves children.

On a different topic, there was the lady Labour Minister of Education whose name eludes me who, on inspecting an institution where the latest TV teaching techniques were being developed, spoke out enthusiastically:

> I am all in favour of short circuit television.

Perhaps she was hoping that it would provide, in the words of another unnamed expert:

> A vast suppository of information.

Name that product

Tastes like grandma – advertisement for a brand of jam

One of the most unfortunate side effects of the global market is the fact that the worldwide community of customers tend to speak a rather large number of different languages, and that attempts by a particular product to extend its sales overseas can fall foul of the language spoken in a particular target market, turning the product into an object of fun or even something entirely undesirable.

Sounds complicated? Not really. Here are a couple of examples.

Once upon a time Rolls Royce decided to produce a new model, called the Silver Shadow, which was manufactured between 1965 and 1980 and turned out to be the most successful of their products.

Originally it was named the Silver Mist, until someone pointed out that, in German, 'Mist' means 'manure' and that such a name might just have a negative effect on sales.

There is also an apocryphal story that Rolls Royce employees were once asked to come up with a name for a new model, and there was a lot of support for the idea of the 'Rolls Royce Andante', until someone opened up Groves Musical Dictionary where the term is defined as 'slowly and without breaks' (read 'brakes' for 'breaks' and you will get the general idea).

By the way, there is actually a travel company called Andante, which presumably doesn't have as its motto the words of Robert Louis Stevenson: 'to travel hopefully is a better thing than to arrive'.

Legend has it that on a visit to Norway, Prince Philip pointed out with much amusement the name of a passing tugboat: Fart. The word simply means 'speed' in Norwegian and Danish, as you may remember from 'fart-kontrol', a Danish speed check road sign, which I cited earlier.

Many of the cars marketed in the UK have such odd names because they are trying to avoid the issues which Rolls Royce faced. Some companies like Peugeot sidestep the issue by branding their marques as 'Peugeot 308', and so forth, and other manufacturers perform similar tricks with 'Series 3' and the like, but others boldly go into the linguistic morass of naming their products.

Would you, for example, drive a Seat Mii? First you would have to pronounce it correctly: 'sea-at', with the emphasis on the first syllable. But it's going a bit far to name a super mini after an avatar you create with the Nintendo Wii games console.

Here are some more unlikely but entirely genuine names:

Isuzu Light Dump

Dacia Duster

Ford Probe

Renault Wind

Beetle RSi

Daihatsu Cherry

KIA

The first offering is a truck, but the name will have it laughed off most building sites; the Duster is, I suppose, a slight improvement on a Cleaning Rag; and the Probe sounds like a painful medical procedure. My daughter bought one second hand, and it developed so many faults I renamed it the 'Prob'.

Passing the Wind, so to speak, it's pretty odd naming a car after RSI, the kind of muscle strain you would get if the steering position was badly designed. That is hardly the brightest idea on the planet; and would you really like to be a young lady reporting to the police station after your Daihatsu had been stolen? ('Please, officer, I have lost my Cherry.')

And as for the KIA, that's US Army jargon for 'Killed in Action'. I suppose a KIA with a faulty satnav would be called a MIA (Missing in Action).

Of course, motor vehicle manufacturers are not the only companies given to baptising their products with unfortunate names. There is no truth in the rumour that the soothing cream Anusol was going to be called 'Bum Sore Wipe' but they came up with this much nicer name.

While we are on this general topic my wife recently purchased one of those perfumed deodorising sprays for the toilet which proudly proclaims on the cover that it contains an electronic 'motion sensor'. Oh, really. Intrusion into privacy has now gone too far.

One of the legendary pratfalls in the product-naming department arose several decades ago from Birds Eye, no less, with a fish product for the kids called 'Cod Balls', which were quietly dropped (no pun intended) from their range. They ought to have called them something entirely harmless like 'Cod Pieces'. Or maybe not.

In a twisted way, I rather like the name of one of the newer products on the DIY scene, the glue which does away with hours of hammering, so it is claimed. It is called 'No more Nails', but to me that sounds rather like the end of a tough day in the torture chamber.

Next up, there is a family fruit jam out there somewhere which actually proudly boasts: 'Tastes like Grandma'. No comment.

Just a few miles down the road from where I am writing, there is a small local winery which produces fruit wines like raspberry, strawberry and a pretty lethal oak leaf wine amongst others. It's called Cairn O'Mohr, and I suspect that the name derives from the fact that after a couple of glasses of Elderberry (at 13.5 per cent) you don't 'care no more'.

That's what I call an appropriate name. I suppose it's matched by Cockburn's Port, which, as someone once said, is like heartburn but a little lower down.

No scholarly survey of product names could be complete without a nod in the direction of Ikea, where there must be a whole company division dedicated to giving their furniture and accessories names which are almost, but not quite, rude. Here are just a few from an inexhaustible supply:

Fartfull – a portable workbench

Fyrkantig – square candles

Jerker – computer desk

That, I suppose, is as good a way as any of ending this particular chapter.

Odds and ends

God answers kneemail – slogan on a Wayside Pulpit

Now, before the chapter on Mr Malaprop, I present a selection of various bits and pieces that don't really fit into any of the other chapters in the book, or if they do, I can't see where to put them. We begin with a wardrobe malfunction from north of the border. After a traditional Scottish wedding, at which most of the male outfits are hired, one attendee was heard to say:

Tomorrow I'm dropping my kilt off in town.

– which calls to mind the Scotsman who, when asked if anything was worn under his kilt, replied:

No, it's all as good as new.

I believe the tactful way to avoid posing that question is to look at his shoes to see if there is dandruff on them.

Now some advice to those of you who have friends with unfortunate names. If you are attending an exhibition of English landscape paintings and see an American friend, don't call out: 'Hey, Wayne.' That's with a nod in the direction of Constable's 'Hay Wain'. By the way, if he was such a good painter, why was he never promoted to sergeant? And even more important, when boarding a nearly full aircraft and catching sight of a pal in row 35, please do not shout: 'Hi Jack.'

There used to be a fashion some years ago for boy racers to adorn their Ford Fiestas not just with speed stripes, but also with car windscreen stickers. Here are some examples:

Jack and Jill

George and the Dragon

Kevin and Anyone

Frog and the Princess

Black Jeep of the Family

Jill – Ted

The last item, if you have a twisted mind like mine and run the two words together, comes out as 'jilted'.

In the university world, the study of sociology has for some unaccountable reason been regarded as a less than demanding discipline. (I understand that people are similarly unkind to Media Studies.) And a story which I am told is true concerns the sociology lecturer who was rung up by Radio 2 about giving a live interview on some key topic of the day and was told that there would be a fee. His response? 'Of course, I'll pay!'

One Students' Union convenience boasted a large sign over a toilet paper roll: 'Sociology degrees: please take one.'

Staying for a moment with the lavatorial theme, there are two particular graffiti which are classics of the genre: first, on the toilet door the words 'Beware of limbo dancers', and secondly the rather mystifying writing on the wall in the Oxford union loo: 'Life is just a bowl of fingernails.' And a last flush on the subject comes with an official-looking notice on a toilet door, easily visible only from a seated position:

Now wash your hands.

Now?

A genuine notice from a less than savoury gents public toilet in Scunthorpe many years ago stated:

Gentlemen should adjust their dress before leaving.

Dress?

I turn next to a very mixed bag of bits and pieces. First, a quote in the press about a court case in which a con man was due to be sentenced:

The judge said that he had swindled hundreds of old people.

Next, I am puzzled by the sign in the children's clothing department of a supermarket, into which I wandered by accident: 'Ladybird trousers.' How, I wondered, would they get them over the wing cases? And then back down again?

Nowadays language is changing so fast it's hard to keep up with it, and the meanings of words are shifting at an ever faster rate. Here's a diverting example. The birds in our eaves are making a lot of noise this year, and my wife asked how we can stop them tweeting all night. My answer? Take their mobile phones away.

One political battle in London which has been raging for years is the location of the new runway or airport to combat the current congestion in the airways. A newspaper report suggested that the Prime Minister was contemplating a pretty dangerous manoeuvre:

> Minister prepares ground for Cameron U-turn on Heathrow runway.

I have come across so many diverse humorous phrases or sayings in my search for material for this book that it is hard to select the best. Here are some of my ecclesiastical favourites. There is always a witty turn of phrase to be found on the Wayside Pulpits outside churches and chapels:

> Seven churchless days make one weak.

> Fight truth decay. Brush up on your Bible.

> Ch..ch – what's missing? UR.

> God answers kneemail.

> The meek shall inherit the earth – if it's all right with you.

> Down in the mouth? Try a faith lift.

> Driving yourself too hard? Come in for a service.

On a quite different topic, in a discussion about increasing the maximum penalty for bigamy, one proposal was that there was no need to take any action as the punishment was already severe enough: namely, having two mothers-in-law.

Spoonerisms are named after the university academic, the Reverend William Spooner, who famously mixed up the beginnings of his words. His most well-known example, which takes a little unscrambling, are his parting words to a feckless student:

You have been hissing my mystery lectures and you have tasted one whole worm. You will leave the University by the town drain.

Less difficult to disentangle are these gems of the genre. Advice to a cyclist:

Always ride on a well-boiled icicle.

Next, the unfortunate Master of Ceremonies whose duty it was to introduce the King at a black tie dinner. After months of rehearsing the simple words to himself, he called out at the top of his voice:

Kinklemen, the gent!

An American president was given similar treatment when he was introduced as 'Hoobert Heaver' (instead of Herbert Hoover). And, finally, on a musical note, I quite liked the attempts by one announcer to articulate the title of a famous piece by Delius: 'On cooking the first hero in spring'.

Changing the subject completely: the government has claimed that it had a mandate for approving single-sex marriages. Some wit pointed out that for such solemn commitments you would surely need far more than just one 'man-date'.

Equally unfortunate was the advertisement for recruiting staff for the long-forgotten Laker Airways which included these words:

Must be able to swim.

Perhaps that was to ensure passenger safety en route to America, described by one commentator as 'a land flowing with milk and money'.

We live in an age of constant headlines in the tabloid press about this or that instant cure for everything from cancer to split ends, and on the dangers of salt, sugar, wine and other common food products which the following week turn out to be not so bad for us after all. On Sky News late night review of the next day's press, one contributor was heard to say:

We don't want a sugar tax. It's too much of a blunt

instrument. We need something more granulated.

Indeed we do.

Now for another random selection of quotable odds and ends from various sources. Shopping is one of my least favourite activities and I came across this sad lament from a retail-weary husband:

> When we go to town, we always hold hands. If I let go, she shops.

In the interests of gender balance, here is a woman's response to that observation:

> Cinderella is proof that a new pair of shoes can change your life.

Next, a serious contribution to the challenging subject of sexual orientation:

> If you don't like gay marriage, blame straight people. They are the ones who keep on having gay babies.

And on the subject of marriage, no book of quotations would be complete without a nod in the direction of one of the great exponents of the art, Oscar Wilde:

> Bigamy is having one wife too many. Monogamy is the same.

It is claimed that children nowadays are too sexually aware, but let us assume that the following comment on the marriage of a relative is really due to a lack of expertise in spelling:

> The couple are honeymooning in Grease.

As the bride and groom make their way down the aisle, a child's voice calls out:

> Is he going to shake his pollen on her now?

Equally difficult is the issue of obesity, allegedly one of the great evils of our time. But, according to this chalkboard outside a gastropub, there is another approach to the subject:

> Fat people are harder to kidnap. Stay safe. Eat lots of grub here.

Even better is this nod in the direction of a hit from the Eurythmics, again on a pub chalkboard:

> Sweet dreams are made of cheese. Who am I to disagree?

And the last word on pub notices comes from this sign outside a drinking establishment:

> The liver is evil. It must be punished.

This rather sad comment could have come straight from the pages of *Bridget Jones's Diary*:

> I completely understand how batteries feel because I too am rarely included in things.

I am told that the best way of opening a child-proof bottle top is to find a child to do it for you, and here is another delightful allegedly true example of juvenile ingenuity. Do not try this at home. An impoverished young lad desirous of owning the very latest in printing technology bought a 3D printer, used it to make an identical copy of itself and then sent the original back for a refund.

And to round this chapter off, a hilarious observation from a humourless lady lecturer addressing a bored gathering of students on the subject of materials for use in dress design and decoration:

> Don't tell me it's difficult to get hold of felt. I can get felt any time I go down the High Street.

A man of his word – Mr Malaprop

I am sorry to say...that my affluence over my niece is very small -
Mrs Malaprop in *The Rivals*

Many decades ago, in a northern English university, there was a much-loved individual who had a very unfortunate way with words. Colleagues carefully catalogued his not so bons mots over many years, and I was involved in that noble enterprise. Now that the gentleman concerned has departed this linguistically challenging world, I can reveal the major jewels in his foot in mouth crown.

But first an explanation of who the original Mrs Malaprop was and what her perverse talent might be.

Mrs Malaprop is a character from Richard Sheridan's first play *The Rivals*, who mangles the English language while remaining totally unaware of her inappropriate utterances. At the same time, her words are close enough to the proper meaning to make sense to the listener. Here are a couple of splendid examples from her extensive repertoire: 'Promise to forget this fellow – to illiterate him, I say, quite from your memory.' And casting aspersions on Lydia, another character in the play: 'She's as headstrong as an allegory on the banks of the Nile.' (She means 'alligator'.)

The person delivering these mutilated words and phrases seems to be oblivious to them like the Mayor's wife who blithely tells her guests when discussing repainting the Town Hall that they should use Durex, as she and her husband had used it for years and it had never let them down. Another civic dignitary, railing against people making false accusations against him, asserted, 'I am sick of these allegations and I am happy to confront the alligators.' Taoiseach of Ireland Bertie Ahern famously warned his people against upsetting the apple tart (otherwise you'd presumably end up with tarte tatin).

There is also a Shakespearean character, Dogberry from *Much Ado About Nothing*, who was born with a silver foot in his mouth. Here are some samples of his linguistic infelicities. 'First, who think you the most desertless man to be constable?' In fact, he is after the most *deserving* man for the role. (I have just accidentally miskeyed 'deserving' and was offered 'windsurfing' as one of the options.) He also informs us that 'Comparisons are odorous'. And, in a disapproving outburst against Count Claudio:

> O villain! thou wilt be condemned into everlasting redemption for this.

Everyone has at least one moment like this. A former secretary of mine was a lovely lady who often proclaimed, 'Some people say things and they don't realise what they are saying.' Her own best foot in mouth moment came after I had congratulated her for being very clever in anticipating my request for some important documents. Her reply came without a hint of irony:

> It makes up for my boobs, you know.

The rest of this chapter is devoted to the linguistic manglings of our genuine Mr Malaprop.

On the subject of weeding a graveyard he asserts: 'No problem. You just spray the stones with parakeet twice a year.' (The correct name of the herbicidal poison he is referring to is 'paraquat').

An intractable problem overcome: 'I dug my heels in but it took a bit of getting round.'

About a colleague with a persecution complex: 'I think he's a panaroic.'

Referring to Buitoni: 'Yes, that's the best forgetti you can buy.'

A colleague had problems sorting out travel to the Middle East: 'He's going to Saudi Arabia as soon as he gets a visor.'

Here he is referring to negotiations on industrial relations: 'Taking arbitrary action.'

Our chronicler believes the following is a mash-up of coup de grâce and fait accompli: 'I would be presented with a coup de fay.'

He offers an unambiguous description of his approach to catering for functions: 'I condense the potential and then hit it with everything I've got.'

He runs a busy lunch service: 'At lunch time my staff are skating about like dynamite.'

But he isn't too sure about the sandwiches: 'I am floating a little on the cold table.'

Firm action, then a budget offering: 'I threw the book at them and put it on a shoestring.'

Coping with staffing arrangements (at least I hope that's what it means): 'I am prepared to attempt service with three staff, one of which will be syphoned from upstairs.'

On the subject of the exclusive nature of the academic staff area: 'The Senior Common Room cannot have open sesame for divers reasons.'

This bon mot ought to be part of standard English: 'If they call the tune, they must stand the racket.'

Scientific information about a colleague recovering in hospital: 'The post-operative body is nitrogenously starved.'

Noses to the grindstone, backs to the wheel, eye on the ball and best foot forward: 'We must let in our gears, get down to brass tacks and not cry for the stars.'

The idea caused a problem but it worked: 'The balloon went up, but it held water.'

Nasty habit this, stains the gills, but quite useful as a book title: 'She smokes like a fish.'

Staffing problems: 'The Staff refectory is often inhibited at the weekends.'

No change, then: 'They decided to let the status quo remain as it is.'

This actually sounds better than Lebensraum: 'I need what Hitler needed – more Liebestraum.' (Just in case: 'Liebestraum' translates as 'dream of love', and is the title of a piano piece by Liszt. 'Lebensraum' means 'living space' and was used by Hitler as an excuse for territorial expansion, especially in Eastern

Europe.)

To someone suffering from an eye problem: 'You've got a scar on the cortina.' (Cortina was a well-known marque of Ford cars at the time.)

Quoting for an evening function: 'An inclusive price for the above dinner including premandial sherry.'

Occasionally he came up with totally inscrutable utterances. Here are just four of them:

'This is causing undue realism.'

'The new service will be more virulent.'

'Food is one of the most insidious things there is.'

'We will provide laminated sandwiches.'

Now for a learned discourse on the size of bowls: 'Soup bowls, I prefer the standard type of soup bowl, which we call cereal, which can be used for soup, cereals and the consequent benefit of standardisation against the weight.'

A good compromise: 'I'll commiserate with you for 45/-.' (For the younger generation, that's forty-five shillings in old money, or two pounds five shillings. In decimal money, that's two pounds twenty-five pence.)

Never mind the plates, just serve the food: 'From a suitably sited point, the soup can be served direct to the covers.'

Looking back, a lack of tubers was the cause of the problem: 'A retrospective shortage of potatoes.'

A free hand: 'They gave me carche blanche.'

As they say, the English can only see the writing on the wall when their backs are up against it: 'When I have my back to the wall, I squeeze everything.'

A fascination with temperature levels, presumably for preserving food: 'I don't care whether they're F or C, so long as I get 5 degrees!'

An excellent reaction: 'The response has been just fanatic.'

Commenting on a coffee break where little of the food was eaten, our Mr Malaprop remarked that there had been a 'dissension from biscuits'.

In relation to the international oil embargo of 1973: 'Someone is playing fox and glove with this one.'

About a troublesome cleric: 'It's the vicar who's the cause of the trouble. He's the kitten in the woodbine.'

Probably intending to encourage swift action when the proverbial fertiliser hits the fan: 'Clear the decks as soon as the dust rises.'

But it won't be available until it's available: 'It will be ready as soon as it's ready.'

History does not record what he is referring to here (thankfully, perhaps): 'It looks bigger than it is.'

A comment about student finances which – we think – means they don't like putting their hands in their pockets: 'Students are susceptible to visible expenditure.'

Plans for a dinner, which thankfully isn't for Norwegians: 'I'm putting on a dinner for Glasgow-wegians.'

At least he didn't fall for a fast one: 'I was too slow to fall for that one.'

Take all the figures into consideration and you'll get this clear as mud result: 'The multiplicity of those documents in aggregate gives me the figure.'

As he was about to retire, he made a clarion call to action: 'In view of my eminent departure, condense it and hit it with all you've got.'

Money is coming in (I think): 'My income is so solid that I have to revert and precost to get any tolerance.'

About preparing for the mid-morning break: 'The pre-milking of coffee cups.'

A parting shot about his use of language: 'You must excuse my metaphorics.'

And the one-liner which sums it all up: 'It's something you say rather than put into words.'

The most challenging part of gathering these gems was (a) keeping a straight face when the lines were delivered and (b) remembering in the explosion of subsequent mirth what it was that he had actually said and duly recording it for posterity, because, as Mr Malaprop might have said, 'What has posterity ever done for me?'

My anecdotage

Tell me, was it you or your brother who died in the war? College Master allegedly questioning a graduate during Open Day.

The following unkindly words were said of a former University Vice Chancellor: 'He's not in his dotage, he's in his anecdotage.' Now in my own anecdotage, I offer a few episodes from my fairly chequered career. I have been known to open my mouth during lectures and place my foot in it.

Two of my better efforts are these: a reference to 'the baby Mozart in the bullrushes' (I meant Moses, of course) and a quote about the character of Herod in a nineteenth-century German play: 'His life can be divided into two parts: in his public part he was most successful.' I leave you to work out how I completed the statement. I turn now to a selection of more substantial offerings.

Writing for the *Times Literary Supplement*

When I started reviewing for the *Times Literary Supplement (TLS)* at the beginning of the 1970s, one of the key features of that august weekly was that reviewers should remain anonymous. It was believed at the time that this decision allowed them to ply their trade without fear or favour, a practice which, as you will see later, had rather awkward consequences for me when it was suddenly changed without warning.

Anyway, in the days of the anonymous reviewer, I was approached by a lady member of my German literature evening class in York (who shall remain, like the reviewer, anonymous) who told me that it was a pity I had not been able to attend the lecture the previous week by the celebrated East German poet Peter Huchel.

And had I read the brilliant review of his latest volume of poems in the *TLS*? I was fortunate to have the following reply at my disposal:

Read it, madam? I wrote it.

That was one of the very few occasions on which I had the opportunity to indulge in a little one-upmanship.

Then, after one-upmanship, came comeuppance.

I had been given to review the *Dictionary of German Synonyms* by a distinguished Professor of German and I did not like it one little bit, not least because it was very selective and personal, qualities which are not exactly to be expected in a work of reference.

The indexing also left a lot to be desired. I still have the yellowing cutting of the review, which concluded:

> The *Dictionary of German Synonyms* coyly abbreviates the titles of the various Oxford dictionaries it consults as COD, POD and SOD respectively, and one is half tempted to wonder whether anyone driven to consult this work could be described as having gone to the DOGS.

Unfortunately, this review appeared just after the editorial policy of reviewer anonymity had been reversed, but even more regrettably, no one had thought to inform the reviewers that this momentous volte face had taken place.

Fortunately for me, the Professor concerned was at that time resident in Australia, but I still double check the door locks at night. (The abbreviated three Oxford dictionaries referred to were, respectively, the Concise, Pocket and Shorter.)

My trade union days

At Hull University, I was for some years secretary of the local Association of University Teachers (AUT) branch. The issue of pay was a long-running sore. Lecturing staff had annual increments which as the years went by ceased to be little more than cost of living increases, so I rebaptised them as excrements.

On several occasions our local branch engaged in a suitably restrained form of industrial inaction, which involved a small group of demonstrators standing outside the main entrance to the university waving banners.

I recall our local AUT President holding up a sign with the legend 'Campus Interruptus', much to the bafflement of passers-by. His other attempt at sloganising was equally abstruse: 'Rectify the anomaly', referring to discrepancies in salary differentials. When asked what the main attraction of a university lecturing career might be, I would always reply: 'A profound dislike of money.'

On the plus side, so the claim goes, it is almost impossible to sack a lecturer. The standard definition of grounds for dismissal goes something like this: being caught having sex with the Vice Chancellor's wife in public – during term time.

And there's one more little gem from my trade union involvement. There was a serious storm in a teacup over a national policy initiative to inject funds to increase the number of younger lecturers and counterbalance the issues arising from 'incremental drift'.

This term relates to the paradox which occurs when recruitment is frozen. Instead of decreasing, the salary bill actually goes up, caused by the fact that people get older, automatically move up the salary scale, and cost more as they do so. The memo sent out about this new initiative was, without a breath of irony as to its sanguinary implications, entitled the 'new blood letter'.

A comment from Philip Larkin

I cannot end my anecdotes without a reference to another review for the *TLS*. I was offered the unique opportunity to review the *Index Expressionismus*, a pioneering computer-based bibliography of German Expressionism of which I was given the only review copy. It weighed in at eighteen massive volumes and the critical assessment was to take pride of place in the *TLS* centre page spread.

I was greatly looking forward to the task, not least because I had been taking a leading role in early experiments with computing and language learning.

Unfortunately, the *Index* turned out to be something of a disaster, to put it mildly, so much so that I recall the *TLS* had to summon the company lawyers to go through my review with a fine tooth comb. Eventually the article appeared, mercifully still back in the days of anonymous reviewers, and on publication day I recall walking along what was known in Hull as the Great White Way, the wide pedestrian path which runs right through the main campus, when the University Librarian, Philip Larkin, the greatest Poet Laureate we never had, accosted me.

Using the custom of addressing a colleague by his or her surname, Philip said to me, 'Do I detect your delicate tone, Last?'

Indeed he did.

And to end it all...

I conclude with a sentence in the details for a University Politics and Russian Studies course, once more in a northern university which shall remain nameless. In documentation of this kind, asterisks and daggers rather than numbers were used to indicate footnotes. The instruction for one footnote ran as follows:

> Insert dagger at the end of course.

Note

I hope you enjoyed this book, and thank you for supporting Guide Dogs.

If you are interested in finding out more about myself and my fiction and study skills eBooks, please read through the next few pages, or go to www.locheesoft.com.

Other eBooks by Rex W Last

Title: *Cursing the Darkness*

Category: Fiction

Available from: www.amazon.co.uk

Price: £1.99 (eBook format)

 In Nuremberg, the city which hosted the annual Nazi Party Congresses in the 1930s, a small group of like-minded individuals resolve to try and fight back against the pitiless dominance of the Nazi régime. Like many of his fellow citizens, Dr Johann Voss is tormented by his political impotence and yearns to be able to bring a group of people together to take a stand for decency and humanity. He sees a first opportunity to do so when a strange-looking patient knocks on his door in the middle of the night seeking medical attention for two bullet wounds.

The patient is Rudi, a cross-dressing cabaret comedian with a curious tale to tell, and the group expands further with the recruitment of Thomas, chief mechanic of the city's transport system, disgusted at the cover-up of the killing of a young Jewish girl, and his friend Max, curator of the city's museum and art gallery, who has already been protecting and spiriting away significant works of art looted from Jewish homes.

Daring rescue

Together they embark on a series of daring undertakings: rescuing a Jewish family from a railway wagon in Nuremberg's marshalling yards, dramatically shaming an SS officer who had raped the family's 14-year-old daughter, and causing the spectacular public downfall of an infamous local Nazi aristocrat. Thomas is faced with the threat of death in a concentration camp and Johann is captured by the SS officer whom he shamed for his actions. The group make a courageous attempt to release Johann from the Gestapo interrogation cells.

It is now too dangerous for them to continue on their present path, but their undertakings have remarkable and unexpected consequences.

A touch of satirical humour

This potentially bleak theme is treated with sensitivity and lightness of touch, and although there are dark moments in the narrative, satirical humour plays a central role. The Nazis are caricatured even more than they are demonised, and the reader is left with a positive and life-affirming insight into the resilience of the human spirit when confronted with what appear to be impossible odds.

The title of the book draws on a quotation from Eleanor Roosevelt: 'It is better to light a single candle than to curse the darkness'.

more books>>>

Title: *Wolfgang's Castle*

Category: Fiction

Available from: www.amazon.co.uk

Price: £2.29 (eBook format)

In a remote Bavarian valley in 1940, Nazi scientists are at work on Project Sea Eagle, to create a waterborne war machine which would spearhead a second invasion attempt of Britain. Four anti-Nazi Germans, two SOE operatives and 20 RAF officer POWs set out with severely limited resources and considerable ingenuity to destroy this 'aquaplane'.

Their target is a hybrid of sea-going craft and airplane which exploits a phenomenon called the 'ground effect', which enables the vehicle to 'fly' a few feet above the water surface at very high speeds with minimum drag.

Destroying a super weapon

The design and production facility for Sea Eagle is housed underground, making it inaccessible to a bombing raid – and in any event a large-scale military assault would be out of the question, given the logistics, the unacceptable potential loss of life and the fact that British forces are at full stretch seeking to cope with a rampaging onslaught from an all-conquering Nazi Germany.

Against impossible odds

Major Archie Wellings of the SOE joins forces with the and others in a bold attempt to halt Sea Eagle in its tracks, partly by turning Nazi ideology against itself, but also by a number of extremely clever ruses.

Wolfgang's Castle is the second novel in a loosely-connected series on the challenges facing Germans who were determined to undermine the Hitler régime from within. In the first, *Cursing the Darkness*, some of the characters who also appear in the second novel seek to assist those who through no fault of their own have fallen foul of the régime, and to humiliate some of the worst Nazis in positions of power and influence in the Nuremberg of the the mid-1930s.

The concept of the Ground Effect Vehicle is based on experiments undertaken after the Second World War, some of which actually reached the stage of commercial production. In this novel, it is assumed that the original designs of these vehicles were worked on in Germany in secret in the 1930s and were reaching viability as military weaponry in late 1940.

Challenging issues – from the nature of patriotism to the role of women in wartime – are explored with a touch of satirical humour. It's an exciting and thought-provoking page-turner with a dash of romance.

A third novel in the series, *Operation Seagull*, is under preparation.

more books>>>

Title: *Making Sense of Poetry*

Category: Study Skills

Available from: www.amazon.co.uk

Price: £2.40 (eBook format)

 This plain-speaking introduction to the study and understanding of poetry avoids academic jargon and provides a clear pathway for coming to a deeper awareness of poetry of the present and past ages. The guide is written in a clear and at times amusing style by a long-standing expert in the field.

The guide begins by examining the physical shape of a poem on the page, then moves on to a shopping list of topics:

Vocabulary
Imagery
Point of view
Personalities
Actions
The senses
Position
Rhythm and rhyme
External references
The unexpected

In sum, this is an invaluable introduction to the study of poetry which concentrates on acquiring practical skills.

more books>>>

Title: *Making Sense of Essay Writing*

Category: Study Skills

Available from: www.amazon.co.uk

Price: £2.29 (eBook format)

The task of writing an essay falls into three stages:

> Before
>
> During and
>
> After.

Sounds obvious, but far too many students charge straight into the actual writing without planning and structuring the work required.

Before

First comes the planning process, starting with reading the title of the essay, setting out a plan, and other preparatory work.

If there is a choice of essays, it's essential (a) that you select a topic which suits you and (b) you read the question *very* carefully.

There are various types of essay which vary in the challenge they present to the student:

> description
>
> discussion
>
> evaluation
>
> comparison

Essays should not only be written to the length required, but they must take account of the potential reader(s).

Quotations and bibliographical material should be included where appropriate and set out in the appropriate 'house style'.

And, of course, a prerequisite for any good essay is a sound knowledge of the subject.

During

It's essential that your essay contains the following:

> Introduction
>
> Central section starting with small points
>
> building up to the main point
>
> Conclusion.

The introduction should match the conclusion in length, and (this sounds obvious but it's so often overlooked) the conclusion has to represent a resolution of the issues posed in the introduction.

The guide offers a detailed analysis of how to use good English, namely, style, clarity, punctuation, structure and so forth. The essay should have a cogent and well-organised structure and not consist of a random collection of thoughts thrown together.<p>

After

Finally, after the essay: an extended section on how to check that you have done your best, breaking the process down into individual tasks.

There's also a special section on using the computer to write your essay.

Each part of the guide contains samples culled from the pages of actual student essays.

more books>>>

Title: *Making Sense of German Language*

Category: Study Skills

Available from: www.amazon.co.uk

Price: £3.58 (eBook format)

This is a clear and entertaining introduction to German, aimed at anyone considering studying the language, as well as at those who are fascinated by languages and how they work.

The guide takes an innovative approach by assuming that potential readers bring a great deal of knowledge of their own to the party, starting with German words and phrases which have made their way into English (Blitzkrieg, Dachshund, Kindergarten, to name but three), and with it a fair grasp of how the Germans pronounce their words (Volkswagen, Mozart, etc).

In addition, you will be familiar with how at least one major European language - English - works, and that in itself offers valuable insights into German vocabulary, grammar and syntax.

The emphasis throughout is on explaining why German is as it is, rather than just throwing sets of 'rules' and 'exceptions' at readers and telling them that this is the way things are without teasing out the underlying structures, historical evolution, and compromises which all languages have to cope with.

No punches are pulled: German is not an easy language to master, but it all makes a deal more sense if you are aware of how and why it has evolved into its present form. The main text is dotted with 'interludes', which cover less challenging aspects of the language, like numbers and time, well-known sayings, and compound words.

The guide is rounded off by a number of parallel texts with full analyses.

There are five appendixes:

A pronunciation guide

An extensive glossary of German words and phrases
which have made their way into English

A glossary of technical terms for those unfamiliar with
the jargon of language learning

A brief guide to the German spelling reform – and

Other useful resources.

Printed in Great Britain
by Amazon